Oops!

LEADER~~SLIP~~

Reversing the *SLIDE* of American Enterprise Leadership

Dave Geenens

with Foreword by Stan Toler

dustjacket

ISBN: 978-0-9816017-5-5

Published by:
Dust Jacket Press
PO Box 721243
Oklahoma City, OK 73172
www.dustjacket.com <http://www.dustjacket.com>
800-495-0192

Praises for LEADER*SLIP*

"With the changing workforce, the premise of Dave Geenens' book is accurate. He asserts we need a new type of leadership in the 21st Century and outlines a plan to get us there. Dave's wealth of experience as an executive lends credibility to his writing. It is a practical and must read for the 21st Century leader."

Karen Black, Insight Edge Executive Coaching and Consulting

"*Leader*slip instantly sets itself apart in the realm of business leadership books by boldly declaring that leaders of all kinds are susceptible to the pitfalls created by power, envy, and attention that accompany positions of leadership. Having been the CEO of an Internet technology company for over a decade, I have experienced *Leader*slip*'s* claims of employee power firsthand. It is reality. If you have yet to understand or experience post-modernism, this book will provide you a wealth of information on how to lead the 'zoomer' workforce.

Sean Clouse, CEO, The IQ Group

"Dave Geenens takes his years of extensive leadership experience and blends them with his passion for motivating individuals to bring us a fresh approach to everyday leadership issues. I found myself challenging my approach to issues I act on every day and thinking about how to approach them in new and more effective ways. For years, manufacturing managers have tried to lead by enforcing rules and regulations. Dave challenges us to lead by building trust and enhancing cooperation to better optimize results."

Randy Stabenow, Sr. Vice President of Manufacturing
and Distribution, Gear for Sports/Champion/Under Armour

This book is dedicated in part to the students, faculty, administration, and alumni of Benedictine College in Atchison, Kansas where people work tirelessly and faithfully to change the world by investing in the mind and spirit of young adults.

I also dedicate this book to my wife, Terry; my children, Megan, Aubrey, and Austin; my extended family; my wife's extended family; and in memory of Robert W. (Buck) Buchnowski.

TABLE OF CONTENTS

FOREWORD

I love to pick up a book that challenges my mind and inspires confidence in me as a leader. Dave Geenens' book, Leaderslip: Reversing the Slide of American Enterprise Leadership is a real winner on the important subject of leadership. I know Dave! He's a leader whose work matches his talk. He is a leader who is leading and a writer who knows his topic well from personal experience.

This book is written to help the reader understand the slide of recent leadership in our society. It tracks with other great books that focus on where all the leaders have gone. Without question, leadership in the corporate arena, the church arena and in the political arena has been relegated to the junk heap in so many ways. Dave has hit the nail on the head with this book. He helps even the novice leader understand the path of a developing leader in today's economic climate.

Readers will especially enjoy his legend of the banana peel and the ways he carefully describes the way leaders can influence the actions, thoughts and development of followers.

In this book you will discover principles, strategies, and insights for leadership from a man who has served as CEO of some great organizations. It is a must read for those who want to go to the next level of effective leadership.

Grab a good cup of java and sit down for an entire afternoon and read the newest and one of the best books that I've read in a long time on the subject of leadership.

Remember it's leadership or it's *Leaderslip!*

Stan Toler
Bestselling author and speaker

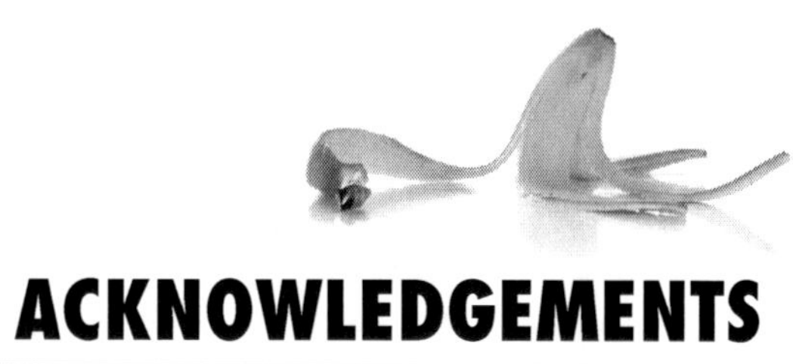

ACKNOWLEDGEMENTS

When I vacation with my family in the Colorado Rocky Mountains, I feel really small. Yet when I return to eastern Kansas, I quickly forget how small I felt against the size and majesty of the mountains. My experience in writing is similar. When I complete a book, my feelings are a blend of relief that the job is done, disappointment that the creative well is dry, and a sense of accomplishment that something worthwhile has been completed. I tend to think of myself as "large" at that time. Then I read and study the works of others. I feel small again.

So many authors, professors, and practitioners have gone before me and, consequently, before this book, laying the ground work for leaders like me to leverage their learning and thinking. I just get to pile on! The likes of Tom Peters, Michael Hammer, Gary Hamel, James Autry, Jim Collins, Patrick Lencioni, Bill Hybels, and Ken Blanchard are just a few. I just glanced through some proof notes for a new book on leadership in the area of law enforcement. Great stuff! I feel small again.

While much credit must go to the aforementioned thinkers and authors, other leaders throughout my career allowed me to practice quite controversial-at-the-time leadership models that produced results. They took a risk that a "new way" might not (produce results). The return on that risk is manifested in this book. John Menghini, Alan Grodnitzky, and Steve Sharpe all let me stretch. They are all big, though, none would admit it.

I must give credit to the two people who helped open my institutionalized eyes to a new truth about leadership: Dr. Jon Hope and Mike Laddin. Though our paths don't cross much, the thinking foundation you gave me is inseparable from the practice of leadership shared in this book.

Many people took the time to read the manuscript, edit its content, and comment on it. Thanks to Randy Stabenow, Karen Black, Tom Bassford, Chuck McGuire, Stan Toler and others who invested in the final product. The final product is better because of you.

Dare I not mention those who gave me enough "me time" to complete a project of this magnitude? Thanks Terry for your support and the "me time."

Most of my inspiration, though, has come from people who have shared the practice field with me; people willing to trust enough in a new way of thinking to step out of institutional norms and do something different. It is their actions that are courageous and validate the concepts and models in this book. To the numerous employees and leaders at Gear for Sports, Impact Design, Penn Emblem, and Avascend, I can't thank you enough for taking chances. Your daily efforts to change the world make me feel very small.

Of course, the God of the universe, my creator, in the person of Jesus Christ, and in the essence of the Holy Spirit, makes me feel small and it is good. Thank you for the blessing of life, breath, supportive friends, talented peers, an unquenchable desire to make a difference, and the perseverance to see a project like this through.

THE LEGEND OF THE BANANA PEEL

What do you expect to be true of a banana peel?

Classic comedy has perpetuated the legend that banana peels, when stepped on, are slippery. Charlie Chaplin, before sound was put to movies, was famous for his falls. The Three Stooges and Woody Allen, stumbling and bumbling along when they happened upon this what-appeared-to-be-harmless fruit carcass, further fueled the slippery legend.

Numerous video games over the last several decades have leveraged this legend to create unforeseen havoc like in Donkey Kong™ and Diddy Kong™ and, again, in Mario Kart Racing™. In all cases, the banana peel causes a slip or a fall that puts you in a disadvantageous position, whether in the lava pit or on the side of the road. Banana peels cause one to slip . . . or so the legend goes.

Have you ever slipped on a banana peel? I haven't, yet I believe the slippery legend to be true; enough so that if I were to happen upon a stray banana peel on the sidewalk, I would give it safe distance, as if it were a spider or a snake ready to strike!

Recently, the legend of the banana peel was tested on an episode of Myth Busters™ on the Discovery Channel™. Guess what happened? A stunt man (actually one of the goofs on the show) tried to walk across a 20-foot platform, from one end to the other, through a coned slalom course. The platform was strewn with banana peels. After 6 falls and a record slow time of 51 seconds to cross the platform, the legend was validated, at least in part. Banana peels are in fact slippery!

Thus, the banana peel is a fitting icon for the subject matter of this book . . .

Beware of banana peels that you find along your path. Otherwise, your time to lead will be monopolized by the constant triage of **leader*slip.*** What may look innocent to the unwary eye can wreak havoc by putting you in a disadvantageous position.

Here is a modern day banana peel proverb:

> "When one comes face-to-face (or foot) with a banana peel, alter your path, else you may find your foot and face in the same place."

PREFACE

No, it's not a typo. Those of us leading business enterprises need only look around, and some of us, only in the mirror, to know we have **slipped** as leaders. Either we have slipped or the world has slid beneath our feet. Regardless of origin, our pace of leadership change has not kept pace with changes in the world and, consequently, our effectiveness as enterprise leaders is waning.

I am not talking exclusively about the obvious and well-publicized moral and ethical failures of so many leaders in business and other enterprises, though they certainly have contributed to the **slide**. I am talking about the much more subtle, though no less important, inability to get the workforce of today to engage fully and willingly in the work of the enterprise you lead. Our learned ways aren't working like they used to work. The workforce of tomorrow, which is here today, is different. The pace of change is so quick with the continual introduction of new technologies that planning horizons and strategies must be redrawn multiple times a year. The rest stops along the route seem further apart.

We feel conflicted. Our peers and sometimes our friends (the old, "I have a friend who . . ." line) have gotten caught up in the prestige, the pride, and the greed that tempts all of us as leaders of profit-making machines. Envy and attention follow "champions of enterprise" as our Boards, shareholders, and industry peers shower accolade upon accolade, both quantitative and qualitative, on us as competitive winners in the cut-throat world of business. We are modern-day gladiators to many, if only for the envy others have of the rewards we reap on the backs of other people.

The investor crowds love us. Like some who reach celebrity quickly, all the attention as a successful business executive can be both titillating and awkward. Like some celebrities, some of us bemoan and laugh-off the attention we get from admirers. Others of us relish the moments when we have the spotlight, while others curse the intrusion of the media or paparazzi. Isn't there something inside all of us that envies the special kind of attention business executives get? We feel powerful, don't we?! We all like to be recognized. We all like to be held-out as a champion. Power, envy, and attention are addictive and, whatever their nature, are causal to the **slip** and **slide** of our enterprise leadership. These are some of the many proverbial banana peels that can trip us up along the way.

The admiration of others can rarely be attributed to any kind of positive press coverage. Most of the press covers plant closings, union votes, ridiculous severance packages, layoffs, etc. Even the good news of record profits or dividends yields a response from the court of public opinion like, "Yeah, at the expense of whose job or life?" Yet, our friends, peers, churches, and fellow philanthropists continue to shower us with this undue and undeserved admiration, perpetuating the **slip** and the **slide**. Because of these high expectations, many of us feel extraordinary pressure to conform and to hide any hint of problems with how or why we do things; staying the course, if for no reason other than to not disappoint those who revel collaterally in our success. The benefits of staying the course far outweigh the risks of changing who we are and, consequently, what we do.

Recently, I was teaching a Strategic Management class at Benedictine College. This is a group of Business School seniors in their last semester before graduation. I asked the class to define leadership and to name some people who are or were great leaders. Dr. Martin Luther King, Jr. made the list as you might imagine. Mahatma Ghandi made the list. No surprise there. Even Adolf Hitler made the list (for reasons of getting people to follow, not for his perverse and detestable strategies against the world's Jewish population)! Noticeably absent from their list was a business leader. Any business leader. Does that seem odd to you? In this group of graduating business majors, not one named a single business leader to their list of great leaders!

I challenged the class to think of some outstanding business leaders. After minutes of pondering, the only two they came up with were Steve Jobs of Apple Computer and Bill Gates of Microsoft. Good choices; highly visible . . . but is that it?! Does a leader's visibility equal his or her leadership? Apparently we business leaders don't make much of an impression even when the judges are stacked in our favor from one of the best business schools in the country?! Might I submit this phenomenon as *exhibit number one* that our leadership as business executives has **slipped**? Little of what we business executives do rises to the level of what others would view as stellar leadership.

Some of you may be reeling right now, because you associate this **slide** in business leadership to others, not to yourself. Need we paint a scarlet letter on all business leaders and executives? Well, the fraternity to which all of us belong as business executives is small and, whether we like it or not, draws us into the same company as Ken Lay of Enron, Bernie Ebbers of WorldCom, and one Bernie Madoff. Need I say more?! If not guilty in fact, we are certainly guilty by association. This is *exhibit number two* supporting our leader***slip***.

While the investor crowds love us, the employee crowds, at best, tolerate us, and at worst, despise us. Is this what business leadership reaps; hoards of employees who believe we are self-centered, arrogant, in-it-for-the-money, and willing to profit at-all-costs?! Am I too harsh? Perhaps. Surely there are some employees who do more than tolerate their bosses and actually like and respect them. I like to think of myself; my business leadership; as one of these leaders. Who was it that said, "We often judge others by their results, yet we judge ourselves by our intentions?" Hmmmm. Many of us are well intended, but operate in sight of a horizon that is actually the edge of a rut in business and enterprise leadership thinking. Our own employees and their perceptions of us are *exhibit number three* as witnesses to our **slide**.

Most certainly we have slid, slidden, slode . . . you get the point. Here is the scary part. The flawed values and beliefs that perpetuate this **slide** in our business and enterprise leadership are being exposed and exploited by a growing segment of the working population I call the 'zoomers." What are 'zoomers?' 'Zoomers' are the cultural generations beginning with Gen X (born 1965-1979), then Gen Y (born 1980-2000) and Gen Z (2001-present) . . . the whole bunch of them. The truth is 'boomers' are exiting and 'zoomers' are entering the workplace, and the two are diametrically different. We will dive deep in this book to clarify the values and beliefs that drive behaviors in the 'zoomers.' Heed their preferences and their values or surely your leadership **slide** will continue. What is a slope today will be a cliff tomorrow. Your **slide** will become a fall.

You may be wondering what qualifies me to write about enterprise leadership of this new workforce; many of which are young enough to be my kids?! I can't explain it through anything other than timing and perhaps some element of fate or destiny, but I have always felt more closely aligned with the 'zoomers' than with the 'boomers.' I was born in 1960 at the tail end of the Baby Boomer generation or 'boomers.' About the time I began my management career and was learning to lead, Tom Peters was writing about *Thriving on Chaos* and *Liberation Management* and Michael Hammer was writing about *Reengineering the Corporation.* I was lucky enough to hear each author speak in person. What I heard them say was revolutionary and knew it to be true intuitively. Fortunately, I was in a leadership position at a company that was growing very quickly and had the opportunity to put many of these innovative leadership principles into practice. It was an amazing and successful experience by any measure as the company grew 3-fold in 10 years and today still excels as arguably the best in its industry. That initial experience helped transform these principles from mere intuition to cognitive reality for me. I continued to practice, rethink, and redeploy these leadership strategies in other companies in which I led. Results followed. Others have practiced them. Results followed. These proven paradigms and practices are the essence of this book.

Like anything with momentum, it will take a strong, consistent counteractive force to first halt the slide; our leader***slip***; then reverse it. This book is written for that precise purpose. Of course, a solution without a problem does no one any good. We will define the core problem behind the **slide** in our business and enterprise leadership. A problem well-defined is half solved. This will allow us to be surgical with our practical and essential solution; offered not just in theory, but in the practical application of leadership at work. Ultimately, the choice will be yours to exact change in your leadership practices where you work and lead.

In 2008, author and Visiting Professor of Strategic and International Management at the London School of Business, Gary Hamel, introduced his book, *The Future of Management.* The Wall Street Journal™ named him as the most influential business thinker of our times. In this book, he makes a point of emphasizing the rut in which we business leaders work and the necessity of leadership and management innovation. I couldn't help but draw comparisons to what I had read from Peters and Hammer in the '80's. It was déjà vu all over again – for you Yogi Berra fans! In many ways, it's the same advice 25 years later. Leadership change is essential if our enterprises are going to compete in the 21st century. This brings us to our *fourth and final exhibit* that our leadership has **slipped**. The truth is our incremental gains over the last 25 years have been outstripped significantly by the pace of change in the world and the influence of cultural generations inhabiting the world. We have not adapted enough, and have, consequently, placed our enterprises in peril.

Gary Hamel writes in *The Future of Management*, "Put bluntly, there is no way to build tomorrow's essential organizational capabilities atop the scaffolding of 20th-century management precepts." The infrastructure on which current leadership practices are built, including values, beliefs, and paradigms must change if we are to lead our enterprises to sustained success in the 21st century. But we must first stop the slide of our enterprise leadership; then reverse it. The answer is a-very-important few pages away. The work to change will be hard, but the rewards that await you and the stakeholders of your enterprise are spectacular. "A pearl of great price is not to be had for the asking." Similarly, **leadership of a different kind** is not gained by simple request or wishful thinking. It is hard work and the work begins now.

Enjoy the book. Enjoy the work. Enjoy the peace and prosperity that comes when people fully and willingly commit to the work of the enterprise you lead.

DEFINING THE PROBLEM

"The rallying cry of Karl Marx in his Communist Manifesto was, 'Workers of the world unite!' He was speaking to the heart of the proletariat, or the working people pitted against the bourgeoisie, or the wealthy and privileged. Leading up to the Bolshevik Revolution, the working class of Russia had reached their boiling point with leaders in their country.

There is a more subtle, yet no less powerful revolution brewing in the United States. The revolution has just begun. Though young, its influence is being felt in work places all across America. Enterprises of all sizes have begun to struggle with its manifestation. The weapon being used by the oppressed, the worker, against the oppressor, the leader, is not a gun, a bomb, or a biological weapon. The weapon being used to bring the oppressor to his or her knees is CHOICE."

Dave Geenens

The risk of opening a book with a comment about Karl Marx's Communist Manifesto is that readers will immediately view the writing as an endorsement of some form of Socialism. Nothing could be further from the truth. This book is intended for leaders who daily practice in the world of pure, unadulterated Capitalism; like that which exists in the United States. This book is written to address an uprising in the workplace that is having profound effects on enterprises in this capitalist economy. The 'zoomers' are rising! If you are a capitalist who wants to produce better, more optimal results, you must read on, because your failure to do so could mean the death of your enterprise.

The working world has changed, and the workers have changed it. The balance of power has shifted from the owner or manager to the worker. As the manufacturing base of the U.S. economy has dwindled and the service sector of the U.S. economy has exploded, catalyzed by the Internet and related technologies, knowledge workers have garnered the keys to the kingdom. Technology today is inseparable from the processes and competitive advantage or simple sustenance of an enterprise. The Internet has made information, especially comparative information, from price to specifications, available at one's finger tips. This knowledge is easy to get and is often free. The sales/buyer relationship has taken a beating on the heels of this information tsunami. Who needs a sales person when product or service expertise is accessible in minutes on the Internet?

The consumer is much more informed. So is the worker. Where technology has become a competitive advantage, the worker in whom the development knowledge resides is the asset. Where knowledge is readily accessible and free, the worker is portable to move and work wherever and whenever he or she wants. In both cases the worker is in control and carries the weapon of **choice**. And the 'zoomers' know it.

Today's employees want more flexibility in their schedules. Early risers want to work at the crack of dawn until early afternoon so they can enjoy their late afternoons or pick up their kids from school. Night owls dare not start their day until noon, so that "after work" comes just in time for happy hour with their friends. Work from home, you say? Absolutely! Today's employees want to work at something they enjoy. They seem to have this natural inclination that life is short and meant to be enjoyed. Consequently, why would they work at something that doesn't deliver satisfaction? Often times, today's employees don't seem to have the drive or ambition that you or I had. They don't seem to be as serious. Their drive and commitment comes from something other than a paycheck. They want to wear what feels comfortable. Open shirt tails and flip flops help "open the mind" for creativity and ingenuity. Tattoos and piercings are simply personal body art not intended for you or me to judge. It's art! All of these new employees know how to use technology and love to use it, whether for productive or less-than-productive purposes. On-line with iPod in ears is nirvana for the 'zoomers'. Many 'zoomers' would rather make less in order to experience a workplace like this. Welcome to the workforce of the 21st Century! Welcome to the world of the 'zoomers.'

Yet our enterprises roll on. We make slight changes in our work place in an attempt to attract new workers, but substantial change is just too counter-cultural and scary to implement. We give raises when policies demand it or when we feel like it. Our policy manuals are like stone tablets, only updated when a law changes that makes us revise something. Many of our processes date back to the days of batch processing and mass production. We hire low and give lip service to employee development. We expect loyalty yet offer none in return, making changes that are chalked up as "just business." We accept the rights and privileges that come with leading an enterprise and act as if we are entitled to the wealth that is generated strictly for the benefit of shareholders; at least that is what we are taught. We lead with a top-down view of the world and expect others to follow out of respect for our position or in response to the weight of our hand. Perhaps this is over-dramatized a bit, but it is much too close to the truth.

In order for the workforce of the 21st Century and the enterprises of today to meet, something must give. If you are turning over rocks looking for the last few eternally loyal, come-to-work-everyday, wear-the-uniform, collect-a-check-and-be-thankful, and just-do-the-work people, you are chasing a ghost. The workforce of the 21st Century is not going to give. There has been something resembling a tectonic shift in the underlying value system of today's workers; the 'zoomers.' It has been evolving for decades and now it has arrived. It is commonly known as post-modernism.

Post-modernism is a confusing term to me. I have always thought the word modern to mean the latest and greatest; the newest or most refined. Modern makes me think of "edgy" things; contemporary architecture and the like. When you stick the word "post," meaning "after," before modern, it points to something after the latest and greatest or the newest. It's past the "edge." My brain has a hard time wrapping itself around something beyond the latest and greatest, and to be honest, it doesn't sound so good. What's past the edge of modern?

We are not the first people to have to deal with this "past-the-edge" question. Innovators for centuries have been asking this question. What did ancient navigators think was past the edge of the world when they thought the world was flat?! I don't think many thought it was good. The edges of ancient maps were encoded with the words "terra incognita," or land unknown. Similarly, I don't think many enterprise leaders think this post-modern age and the related workforce of the 21st Century is going to be good either. It's "terra incognita," for today's business leader.

History, though, gives us some insight into what might happen. When the ancient sailors and navigators of the world realized the world wasn't flat and that there was no edge, a whole new, wonderful world was discovered. New ships were built to take advantage of these unencumbered distances without an edge. New maps had to be drawn. The lure of a new horizon without edges romanced many a man to leave his family and homeland for the treasure beyond. Likewise, you, as a leader, are privileged to be at the beginning of a similar adventure that will prove this post-modern age and the workforce of the 21st Century to be a great workforce, with more talent and capability than any workforce preceding it. But like the ancient sailors, new ships will have to be built and new maps will have to be drawn. The new, wonderful world was not discovered by standing on the near shore. Neither will the workforce of the 21st Century be discovered and leveraged until enterprise leaders change their fundamental beliefs, paradigms, and related behaviors toward leadership. This is the new adventure which every enterprise leader must embrace if success is to follow his or her efforts.

"There has been something resembling a tectonic shift in the underlying value system of today's workers".

This new leadership horizon is exciting to some and very scary for others. Personally, I have been romanced like the ancient sailors to explore and test new concepts that dare to challenge status quo beliefs and paradigms. These concepts of leadership and their practical application will be shared in this book. What I have found is a new, wonderful world where employees commit fully and willingly to the work, whether they are decades-old workers or whether they are poster-children for the post-modern world. I invite you to come along on this journey as we discover together leadership of a different kind for the post-modern world; the world of the 'zoomers.'

Before we begin exploring this new understanding of leadership for the post-modern world, it is important that we uncover and understand that "tectonic shift" previously referred to in the underlying value system of today's workers. If we don't, the dots or map between the new leadership paradigms and the new work world will be blurry, misaligned, and difficult to navigate. Like this current huge shift, the starting point of the modern world in which we have lived for centuries began with a shift from a previous world that I refer to as "truth." Truth, however revealed to and experienced by individual people, existed for a time. During this time, truth was generally accepted as universal, undeniable, incontrovertible, and just "was." Truth was not questioned. It was passed on from generation to generation through ancient and often archaic means of recording. Truth prevailed and the truth was hard. As human beings, we don't like hard truth. When faced with hard truth, humankind is a master at finding ways to make it softer and easier. An example of hard truth is marriage. If you are or have ever been married, you know what I am talking about. "Two becoming one," a common foundation repeated by priests and pastors at marriage ceremonies, speaks to the commitment and reality of marriage. This sounds good, but the practical application of this truth is far from easy and further from automatic.

Human beings are ingenious when it comes to overcoming "hard." Our so-called modern world began with human kind inventing or willing into existence what we now call institutions. This was a tectonic shift from hard truth. When we refer to institutions, don't most of us visualize something strong, stable, venerable, permanent; something for the ages; something that has passed the test of time? We say of something that has persevered, "It has become an institution," and we do so often to cast a positive light on something that has lasted. But is it so good? We as human beings embrace institutions meant to mirror the truth, but that do not require the hard and difficult understanding, communication of, and practice of the truth. For instance, we exchanged the hard truth of marriage for the institution of marriage. The institution mirrored the truth that "two become one," but the truth born out of humility, sacrifice, serving one another, commitment, and loyalty was lost. Today, we can get married in a variety of places, get a marriage certificate, enjoy our relationship while the sex is good, and move on when there might be something better on the other side of the knoll.

Government is another institution man willed into existence. Governing others is hard. It is the ultimate in serving your fellow man and requires a depth and breadth of principle that is rarely seen today. The institution of government is now politicized. Governing is more about position-based authority and pomp and circumstance than it is about projecting and complying with a guiding set of principles.

We have all heard the church referred to as an institution. The church of today is far from the hard truth of everyone selling their possessions and giving to those who have need. Today, it's mostly about one hour a week on Sunday. This is a lot easier than the truth!
Here is the most relevant institution to you as an enterprise leader. Business has also become an institution. Getting others to work together toward a common end has fallen victim to the institutional belief that the purpose of a business is to maximize shareholder wealth. Most businesses I know of were begun to fill a need, first, and at a profit, second. Certainly, if a profit could not be envisioned, the capital was not put at risk, but the need to be filled had to precede profit. The "unmet need" for a business is the hard truth. The focus on the profit to investors is a fruit of the institution.

"We as human beings embrace institutions meant to mirror the truth, but that do not require the hard and difficult understanding, communication of, and practice of the truth".

So how has this modern world, full of institutions meant to mirror the world of truth, been working for us human beings? To quote Dr. Phil, "How's that workin' for ya?" More importantly, how are these institutions viewed by people subject to them? Has not every generation in recent history become increasingly rebellious toward these institutions? I know I was more rebellious than my parents and I know my children are more rebellious than I was. I am not talking about adolescent disregard for authority. I am talking about a calculated and deep rebellion against an institution that *lacks sub-*

stance. Workers today have grown up in a world where marriage is not a commitment, but a convenience; where government is not about principle, but about politics; where faith and religion are not about heart change, but about head knowledge; and where business is not about purpose, but about profit. This is the modern "edge." This is what we have, and what we have has not been acceptable to many for awhile.

The 'zoomers' are coming to finish the battle. Initially, rebellion came in subtle and subversive forms, yet in more recent years, it has come in outright, in-your-face intolerance. The advent of the knowledge economy and the knowledge worker have fueled this intolerance. What once was a grimace of frustration and some prodding of peers in the workplace, is now an immediate dramatic walk off the work site and, using technology, the sneezing of ill-will on everyone within an ear-shot, e-mail shot, or text message. Those of us leading enterprises may view this rebellion as entirely negative; a force meant to overthrow the established norms and behaviors of our enterprise. With this perspective, we are likely to dig fox holes, arm our soldiers, load our weapons and ready ourselves to fight. But what if this force is trying to accomplish something else? **Something good.** Could it be that this rebellion is aimed at the institutions that only vaguely mirror the truth any more, and that the real victory and treasure sought by these rebel 'zoomers' is the sole, hard truth from where our modern world evolved?

As I reflect on my journey as a worker and leader, I believe the latter is true. I want a government leader who leads from an undeniable set of principles, not from political aspirations or loyalties. I want to be a man fully committed to my wife in marriage and not just a shell-of-a-man who drifts in the wind; a man who will fight for his family. I want to give meaningfully to the poor and live for something bigger than what this world has to offer. Finally, I want to know and understand the purpose for which a business was born. I don't care about the wealth of the shareholders, even if I am one! The truth is nobody else in our enterprise does either. People don't work to see someone else get wealthy. They do it to participate in something meaningful and rewarding. If wealth is a by-product of doing something well, so be it. But it is certainly not the purpose that gives rise to commitment at work.

"Has not every generation in recent history become increasingly rebellious toward these institutions?"

So where does all this leave us as leaders, other than scared and standing on the near shore? Is hard truth something to fear or something to embrace? Long ago we abandoned the hard truth with the advent of institutions. The workforce of the 21st Century, the 'zoomers,' are forcing us to go back from where we came. They are pushing us to purpose them. They are expecting us to lead them in ways that inspire them and release them to perform at their absolute best. And if we don't, they will refuse to fully and willingly commit to the work, significantly affecting enterprise results. It's already happening all around us.

This new adventure and return to the truth will require us to change the way we lead. We can only change the way we lead if we change the way we think. We can only change the way we think if we change our beliefs. A true tectonic shift has taken place. Believe that your leadership makes a difference. Believe that the best days for your enterprise and your leadership are ahead of you. I extend an invitation to you to join this journey. Together we will courageously leave the near shore for the place where employees of the 21st Century, the 'zoomers,' fully and willingly commit to the work of your enterprise and, with you leading, produce extraordinary results for the benefit of all stakeholders.

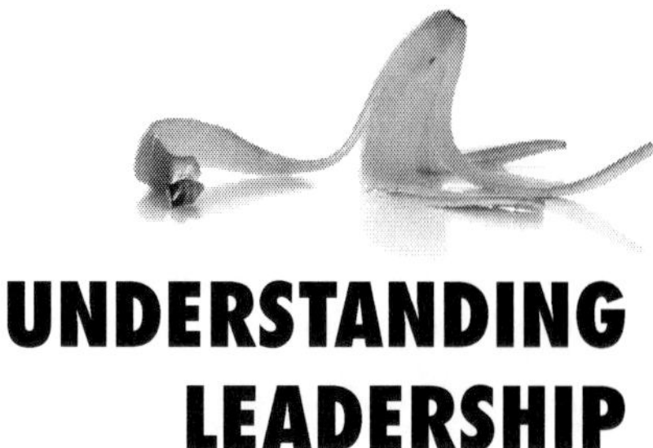

UNDERSTANDING LEADERSHIP

I have read a vast array of authors and prognosticators who believe the future world of business is a model with little or no structure, where leadership is awarded by the workers, and control is significantly decentralized, if evident at all. While I buy some of the concepts like workers having more control, especially in this knowledge economy, I ultimately believe that **leadership of a different kind** will be required to excel in the 21st century, not the abandonment of leadership all together as some might suggest. There still exists a governing dynamic that speaks to the need and essence of leadership in any enterprise. It happens to be found in the Bible in the book of Ecclesiastes, authored by Solomon, widely known and recognized as the wisest man to walk this earth. In Ecclesiastes 4:9, Solomon writes, "Two are better than one because they have a good return for their work." "Good return" is a pure, unadulterated capitalist concept. We will examine and define leadership in light of this governing dynamic that *two are better than one*.

Most of us recognize leadership when we see it, yet a complete definition of leadership is fleeting. Some define leadership as "influencing others." Others define leadership as "getting others to follow." These varied definitions combined with the difficulty of transferring the skills of leaders have resulted in wide misunderstanding and, consequently, misuse of leadership. For instance, people effective at "getting others to follow," have dotted history for millennia. Ancient conquerors organized tens of thousands of soldiers to do their bidding, overtaking lands and pillaging the wealth of civilizations. Monarchs and magistrates ruled ancient communities, organizing them to serve the needs of one another and to protect themselves from rival tribes and communities. More recently and notoriously, the Reverend Jim Jones convinced his followers in Guyana to drink the literal "purple Kool-Aid®" and join one another in death. These people were obviously successful at getting others to follow, but did they lead in order to accomplish this feat? Let's look deeper at what might be interpreted as leadership.

There are many ways to "get others to follow," other than leading them. It's amazing how threatening someone will work! Most of us have experienced the "quid pro quo" demands at some point in our work life. "Do this or else . . . (you fill in the blank)!" Withholding things others need is also a way to extort effort from someone. Some managers hoard information in order to control the behaviors of the people they are charged with leading. By controlling access to tools we can get others to wait on us before they begin their work giving us control over their work pace and performance. This is a form of controlling information. If all else fails, providing an undesirable option for abandoning the effort will certainly get others to follow. "If you bail out on us now, we will leave you out and alone." Ambiguity can create tyranny; an environment where people are afraid to do anything unless the leader says to do something. Saddam Hussein was known as a tyrant. His ambiguous treatment of people caused others to do absolutely as he commanded. His history told people he would probably kill them if they did not do as he had requested. That same fate would even await some who did just as Hussein said as they might be viewed as "weak." Either way, there was chance that one might perish, so most did nothing to draw attention to themselves and if he did ask them to do something, they would do it simply to lessen the odds of retribution.

We see similar means like these used in the marketplace to get people to follow all the time; holding up a meeting intentionally just so people realize who is really important and necessary to the process; barking loudly to disguise a lack of competency that co-workers know exists; hiding critical data from others doing the work so that one can garner all the credit. Is this leadership? No. Words used to represent these methods include intimidation and manipulation. Do these methods produce results? Yes, some.

If you define leadership as simply "getting others to follow," you open the box of means to include many methods that can produce some positive results, but are not leadership. In fact, many of these means are very tempting to use because they often produce quicker results, are easier to use, and leave a residual effect in the form of legends that last well beyond the immediate impact of the use of the method itself. Intimidation and manipulation have a way of lingering in the minds and hearts of those who have witnessed and been subjected to their use.

The days of executives intimidating and manipulating workers to get results are quickly becoming lore. At a time when workers were many and options were few, these means produced some results. Today, though, where the worker is more in control, other means are required to produce optimal results. Even in an economy where options are shrinking with the recession or depression of 2009, employees are unlikely to abandon their rebellion against institutions, and if they do so only to get a job, you will get an employee who is far from fully committed to the work.

Much has been written in the last few decades trying to educate enterprise leaders of the work of leadership, and the means today that get others to, not just follow, but fully and willingly commit to the work or effort. Without a new understanding of leadership, though, many executive leaders struggle to abandon the means that are easier to use, quicker to deploy, and that persist, even in the leader's absence.

The world has also changed under our feet. The new, commonly referred to as, "post-modern" thinking practiced by the 'zoomers' poses more obstacles to getting others to fully and willingly commit to common work or effort. People entering the work force with this thinking lack significant, if not total disregard for institutions, including businesses and enterprises, that only vaguely and distantly represent the original purpose for which they were formed. For example, businesses in the United States organized to build the infrastructure of this country are now viewed as and function as institutions that exist primarily to produce wealth to shareholders. The original reason for their birth is long forgotten and clouded by the weight and structure of the institution. The railroad industry is a good example. There was reason and purpose beyond money and wealth that birthed the "iron horse" idea. The continental U.S. was greatly unexplored and certainly unsettled. Adventurers and frontiersmen forged trails, set up outposts, and began communities. These communities needed resources with which to build infrastructure and deliver products to the ever-growing multitudes of people venturing west. Many of the factories and resources were in the east. How would the resources get to the west? What would have happened had someone not dreamed of the steam locomotive pulling tons of resources to those in need? This is a plausible idea of what birthed the modern railroad industry in the U.S. Do we ever talk or think about that anymore, or do we just check out the company stock values on the latest index report?

Committing to an institution like this is not part of "post-modern" thinking. 'Zoomers' seek the truth clouded by the institution. In order to engage this generation, an executive must go back to the reason for and truth underlying the existence of the enterprise. This is not only an invitation to practice leadership of a different kind, but it is a practical necessity as the void left by aging 'boomer' enterprise leaders must be filled by these new-thinking, truth-thank-you-very-much, 'zoomers.'

Before we get to a new definition for and understanding of leadership, let's examine leadership's application in a variety of enterprises. One of the premises of leadership is that, before leadership is required, the work must require more than just you. This is true, isn't it? Must you concern yourself with other people engaging in the work if you can do all the work yourself? No. Leadership is not required as long the work requires just you. As soon as the work requires more than just you, leadership is absolutely required in order to optimize results and outcomes. Remember the *two are better than one* governing dynamic.

The term "enterprise" is commonly used to represent an entity where the work requires more than just you. A business where the work requires more than the entrepreneur/founder is an enterprise. A school where there is more than one teacher is an enterprise. A government where there is more than one official is an enterprise. A church where someone other than the priest, pastor, rabbi, or cleric is required to do the work is an enterprise. This leadership premise applies to any and all enterprises.

"Leadership is not required as long as the work requires just you. As soon as the work requires more than just you, leadership is absolutely required in order to optimize results and outcomes."

Leadership not only applies to all types of enterprises, but it is independent of the type or context of the work. If making pizzas is the nature of your business and the work requires more than just you, then leadership is required to optimize results. If building high-tech global positioning devices is the nature of your business and the work requires more than just you, then leadership is required to optimize results. If insuring others against property/casualty losses is what you do and the work requires more than just you, then leadership is required. If providing resources and spiritual comfort for those in need is the nature of your work and the work requires more than just you, then leadership is required.

It is critical that we not take lightly the transition from the work requiring just you to the work requiring more than just you; **the formative point of an enterprise.** As an entrepreneur or founder, you began your one-day-to-be-an-enterprise with a mission and vision to accomplish results and outcomes that matter. You committed yourself to overcoming the many obstacles to success, even if that meant you had to perform all the tasks as the proverbial chief cook and bottle washer. Anyone who has had an enterprise vision has likely started this way. Generally speaking, work can be defined as overcoming the series of obstacles to success or desired results and outcomes. If there are not obstacles, then one can argue that effort or work is not required. In enterprises, obstacles to success often include capital enough to fund the effort, skills enough to execute the effort, and materials and tools enough to produce the desired result. If these series of obstacles are not overcome by the entrepreneur or founder, it is likely that the formative point of an enterprise, where the work requires more than just you, will not be reached.

If work can be defined as overcoming the series of obstacles to desired results, what happens when the entrepreneur/founder can no longer do the work by him or herself, yet he or she has all the capital, skills, materials, and tools required to do the work? I suggest to you that at this point the primary obstacle has now fundamentally changed. The primary obstacle is now the entrepreneur's/founder's ability to get someone to work with him or her in the context of the work. The leader's attention and effort, if he or she is going to be successful, must now be directed at getting someone to help in the work. This is not unlike identifying a capacity constraint in a manufacturing process and directing resources to the bottleneck in order to open the throat of capacity to optimize output and throughput. Recognizing this significant change in the obstacle is critical to our new definition and understanding of leadership.

Here is an example of how a versatile, skilled home builder might come face to face with this new obstacle. This home builder is talented and has accumulated enough capital to buy land and build a home on the land, overcoming the first obstacle. The builder is a skilled architect and designer and has submitted and obtained approval of the plans from city officials. The builder has accumulated numerous tools and skills enough to dig the foundation and lay block to build the foundation of the home. The builder uses the capital to secure the wood and nails required to frame the home. Each obstacle to this point has been overcome by the builder himself. The builder proceeds to frame the front wall of the house on the concrete floor; mixed, poured and finished by him alone. The front wall is large and includes headers and a picture window. Now comes the time for the builder to mount and secure the front wall to the foundation. The builder tries to lift the wall, but it's too heavy for him to lift up on the foundation by himself. What is the obstacle? Is it the weight of the wall? No. The obstacle has now shifted to the ability of the builder to get someone to work with him in the effort to lift the wall up on the foundation. Do you see the shift? The obstacle, at the formative point of an enterprise, is independent of the context of the work. Universally, the obstacle at the time the work requires more than just you, is your ability to get someone to cooperate with you in the work. This understanding is the basis for leadership of a different kind.

"Universally, the obstacle at the time the work requires more than just you, is your ability to get someone to cooperate with you in the work."

Taking this obstacle to its logical end, getting others to cooperate in the work is every leader's ultimate goal, because failure to do so limits the results and outcomes to what only you can do alone, which is all but assured to be less than what you can do with the cooperation of others. Remember the *two are better than one* governing dynamic. Failure to get others to cooperate with you in the work is your ultimate obstacle. Leadership is the effort aimed at getting others to fully and willingly commit to the work at hand. In other words, leadership is the art of optimizing cooperation. The word collaboration could be used to describe what needs to be optimized, but collaboration infers a more arms length, separate party relationship rather than the integral, symbiotic relationship normally required to excel at work together. Consequently, cooperation is what leaders are about optimizing.

"Leadership is the art of optimizing cooperation."

This definition and understanding of leadership will change the lenses through which an executive or any enterprise leader views his or her work. The concept of leadership is not complex. It's simple, but the work to get there is hard. Think about some of the decisions you as an executive or enterprise leader have made over the last few years and ask yourself if the decision you made hurt or helped cooperation. Some decisions you have made directly impacted the cooperation of others. Think of a mandate you may have issued, flanked by the power of "it's just business" that you knew was not the right thing to do or how you handled the hiring or firing of a vice president. How would you measure the effect of your action on the cooperation of others within your enterprise?

Some decisions you **didn't** make affected cooperation. Think of a time where you chose not to intervene in a conflict in the hopes that the problem would simply go away, or when you perpetuated a known failure of a colleague because you just didn't want to go there with this one person who had become your friend. Do you think your inaction helped or hurt cooperation?

It is highly likely that many things you do and practice naturally as an enterprise executive affect cooperation; most likely negatively. This blindness, or unconscious incompetence as it relates to leadership and its affect on cooperation, is a proverbial banana peel.

Do the normal and customary perks of an enterprise executive hurt or help cooperation? For example, that parking spot closest to the door marked as "reserved." What do you think the performing employee who parks 100 feet away from the entrance on rainy days thinks of you and your reserved parking spot? Are they more committed to the work after slogging in the rain to work while you enter the building with hardly a drop on you?

As I write this, I am reminded of the last 10 months when the American automobile industry was tried in the court of public opinion. As the 2009 recession began to take shape, the CEO's of the big three American auto makers, General Motors, Ford and Chrysler, pleaded with the U.S. Congress to give them a several billion dollar bail-out. All of them flew to Washington, D.C. in private jets that reportedly cost $15-$20,000 per trip. Do you think Congress might have listened to them more had they flown coach for $300? What about the workers at the factories who watched their friends and neighbors lose their jobs? Do you think they are more committed now knowing their CEO's enjoy a private jet perk, even when the company is failing? Not likely, and the sting of this perk will last awhile, affecting the level of commitment when what the enterprise needs most is the full and willing commitment of its workers to build the best cars at the best prices.

Decades ago, Chrysler went through a difficult time and its CEO at the time, Lee Iacocca, made a similar request of Congress. It was big news and risky, but Congress "loaned" Chrysler the money it needed. In less than the agreed upon term, Chrysler paid back the loan and became a force to be reckoned with in the late 1980s' and '90's. It wasn't just competence that produced this result. Lee Iacocca did an amazing thing in order to align his enterprise for success. What he did next made him one of my early business heroes. He voluntarily cut his salary to $1 a year for two years. For those pundits reading this . . . yes, he was granted large amounts of stock options in lieu of a salary, but those could have been worthless had Chrysler not prevailed. This sent a message to everyone at Chrysler and in Congress, that the leader was fully and willingly committed to the work and that everyone should do the same. This was a key to negotiating savings with the tough auto worker unions and asking others to sacrifice in order to get Chrysler on solid ground for its future. This is a great example of how a leader focused on getting others to cooperate can impact and optimize results. The effort to save Chrysler was bigger than Lee Iacocca and the effort of your enterprise or subset of an enterprise is bigger than you. Lee Iacocca knew he needed others' cooperation in order to be successful. You, too, need to know and live this understanding. Optimizing cooperation is always the ultimate goal.

Another common perk for executives is the executive lavatory or toilet. Now you may think this perk is trivial, but the lenses of cooperation reveal otherwise. Is this perk really necessary? Does this perk help or hurt cooperation? What message does this perk send to others in the enterprise? Is it too much trouble to walk an additional 50 feet to join the rest of the world in a "community," gender-specific bathroom? I believe the message received by others in your enterprise is this: my time is worth more than your time and my excrement doesn't stink. The former may be logically true, but in terms of cooperation, this message certainly has a diminishing effect. The latter isn't true and everyone knows it. Yours stinks, too! If you want to optimize cooperation, put crime-scene tape across the entrance to your privy and join all the others doing the work at your enterprise.

What about your salary? If people knew how much you make, and don't be surprised if they do, would that knowledge hurt or help cooperation? It was disclosed during the big three American automaker hearings before Congress that the CEO of Ford made about $28 million dollars last year. In light of this news, how do you think the line workers at Ford felt about the layoffs executed thereafter? Most people expect and understand that the CEO of a company will earn more than others in the enterprise. Their years of experience, knowledge, and the pressures and accountabilities that come with that job will logically dictate this difference. In many cases, though, what is a logically justifiable difference has become a cooperation-destroying disparity! Optimizing cooperation should rule when determining the leader's salary as well. When coaching executives about their salaries, I use the rule of thumb that says if people found out how much you make, would they be more or less committed to the work? At the point that others would disengage from the work due to an unreasonable disparity in salary, you make too much. Set you salary lower than that point. Heresy you say? Not if cooperation is the ultimate goal! Let me remind you of my comment earlier. The concept of leadership is simple. The work to get there is hard. The decisions a leader must make to optimize cooperation and, ultimately, results, require overcoming many of the ruts worn over decades of paradigms aimed at executive entitlements that accompany the institution of business.

I think you will find that many executive practices accepted as normal and customary in business will often hurt cooperation. Some of you may be feeling offended right now, but remember, we are just being true to the belief that leadership is the art of optimizing cooperation. Making decisions or behaving in ways that diminish cooperation negatively affects desired results and outcomes. The thinking pattern or paradigm change with this belief is significant! If your enterprise is filled with people who do not exhibit full and willing commitment to the work, then check to see how the actions and decisions of the leader have affected cooperation. My guess is that you will find a direct correlation between actions of the leaders and the level of cooperation in the work. Where cooperation lacks, often, true leadership lacks. This concept is not complex, but the work to get there is very hard.

Does this paradigm of optimizing cooperation feel "soft" to you . . . like always optimizing cooperation and the tough decisions required to run a business are incongruent? For example, you may be wondering if letting people go when costs are too high and revenues too low is contrary to optimizing cooperation. You think optimizing cooperation may dictate that employees identified to be let go be retained in order to insure future cooperation, right? Not so fast. In any enterprise, leaders must make tough decisions about the magnitude and use of resources. These decisions definitely effect cooperation. All I am emphasizing is that you, as the leader, be ever diligent and aware that decisions often written off as "just business" have serious consequences to cooperation, and how decisions like this are made and carried out could determine the fate of your enterprise in the future where full and willing commitment of others to the work will be required to compete. Optimal future desired results and outcomes mandate that you no longer be ignorant of the cost of diminished cooperation. True leaders, regardless of the circumstance, optimize cooperation, even if it means that others must leave the enterprise.

"The concept of leadership is not complex, but the work to get there is very hard."

Well, we have now left the near shore for the "terra incognita." How does it feel? Some of you are wishing you never picked up this book and joined this journey. Some of you may be excited about the truth you have read and how to lead with this new set of leadership lenses. In either case, know that there is treasure ahead. Those of you who want to go back, while you are likely fearing the hint of sacrifice or loss to come, know that optimizing results brings a set of rewards that cause what you have already achieved to pale in comparison. And others get to participate meaningfully, enjoying a sense of purpose many felt would never come in the workplace or in their lives. As a result, the commitment of these ‘zoomers’ to something true and real is a competitive advantage that most will find impossible to duplicate.

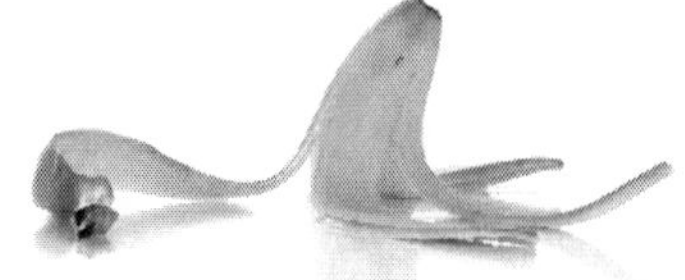

OTHER CONTEMPORARY THINKING

MARCUS BUCKINGHAM

Marcus Buckingham, the rule-breaking author of *Now Find Your Strengths*, extols the benefits to an enterprise and leader when one focuses on the strengths of people vs. over-emphasizing their weaknesses or "areas of improvement." Point well made and taken.

I believe his argument ultimately is about, "Do you shape the work to fit the individual strengths of your people, or do you shape the people to fit the required work to be done?" Anyone with executive experience knows that this is a delicate balancing act. If hiring, firing, and carving strengths in and out of people to create the perfect person for the work or if work could be engineered perfectly to match 100% of the strengths of the people, the world of work would be wonderful. It's not going to happen. The concept of leveraging strengths is great, but the reality is that everyone will have to do something that is not on his or her side of the strength ledger.

His argument, though, leads us to one of the truths about enterprises that we will explore deeply in this book. Here is something to ponder. Is an enterprise, forged out of the bond and commitment of its employees to accomplish something greater than themselves, regardless of individual strengths, **more powerful, attractive, and world-changing**, than a group of people who find personal fulfillment because their strengths are completely honored and leveraged? Honestly, I am not sure the latter is even possible in reality, but I know the former is absolutely possible and necessary in the 21st century . . . but only if one thing exists above all else. That thing is leadership.

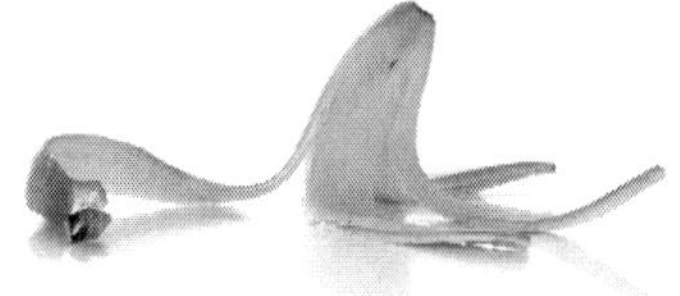

COOPERATIVE COMPETENCY©

True to our new, clear and complete definition of leadership, "the art of optimizing cooperation," we call the measure of a leader's ability to optimize cooperation, his or her *cooperative competency*©. Be careful. The idea that a few nice words and a pat on the back will persuade people to follow is wrong. The 'zoomers' aren't interested in patronizing fluff. Rightly, they are increasingly asking for clarity, truth, and commitment from leadership in return for their dedication and loyalty to the enterprise. To be a competent leader with our new definition and understanding of leadership, one primary goal of any executive is to increase his or her cooperative competency©. This is both hard and humbling work. A highly competent leader is able to optimize cooperation regardless of the circumstance. This will be our goal.

In order to excel at anything of value, practice is paramount. Tiger Woods and Vijay Singh are two of the most diligent, practicing golfers in the world. Is it any wonder that they are the best? Jerry Rice, the hall of fame wide receiver for the San Francisco 49ers, was known for both his aggressive in-season and out-of-season practice routines. Effectively viewing the world of your enterprise through the lenses of cooperation and responding well requires practice. The object of your practice will be your senses and sensitivity to cooperative issues. These new cooperative lenses will likely change the things you see and, consequently, the things you do in response to the things you see. As a result, as your competency increases, you will find people more fully and willingly committing to the work, and, ultimately, optimizing your results.

There are five things effective leaders do; two of which help facilitate cooperation and three which directly affect the cooperative effort in the enterprise. In addition, the way a cooperatively competent leader thinks about problem solving and accountability has a tremendous effect on cooperation. We will review in detail each of the five things leaders do and review an effective model for problem solving and holding others accountable, all of which enhance cooperation when done well. Failure to grasp the importance of these paradigms and behaviors will compromise your ability to reach your goals and achieve results.

Strategic Thinking

The first thing an effective leader does to help facilitate cooperation is **strategically think**. Without the thinking regarding the work and culture of any enterprise, the road to optimal results and outcomes will be rough as those invited to cooperate will not fully understand the nature of the work or the environment in which the work will be done to fully commit. Strategic thinking in the context of cooperative competency© is no different than strategic thinking described in any other context for the benefit of an enterprise, though the focus on optimal outcomes and results through cooperation sheds a different hue on leader activities.

The first question a competent leader must answer is, "What are we doing?" or "What is the work we do?" Answering the "what" question helps a leader define the mission of the enterprise. "We exist to do [what]?" The answer to the "what" question helps dictate the focus of the enterprise and, by intentional exclusion, defines what work the enterprise is not about. At Avascend, one of the companies I led, we defined what we did like this: "We exist to provide service that defies explanation." Avascend is in the healthcare hospitality business, providing a wide array of hospitality services to hospitals and other market segments. The bulk of our business services offered was in valet parking and operating parking structures. We chose not to simply exceed customer expectations. While trite and overused, we expressly excluded this language to define the work we are not about. We wanted words describing what we do to inspire our people to perform extraordinary and spontaneous acts of service. Regardless of the market segment or account, this is how we defined what Avascend does.

Clarifying the mission is the first step in the iterative process of strategic thinking. By iterative, I mean that threading and re-threading of thoughts between steps from mission to accountabilities clarifies activities and aligns resources to achieve the mission. This clarification and alignment is critical to success. These iterative strategic thinking steps can be illustrated this way:

Mission/Vision → Objectives → Strategies → Organizing → Accountabilities

Objectives help quantify and define measures of success for the mission. Strategies clarify activities required to achieve the objectives. Organizing refers to the activity of arranging people and defining decision making authority usually associated with organizational charts. Organizing is a verb and activity critical to the strategic thinking process. Ultimately, to achieve the mission, work and decisions must be assigned to positions and positions must be assigned to people. In order to assign the right person to a given position, the work of the position must be defined and clarified through accountabilities. The accountabilities are usually clarified in a position description.

Sometimes, when a mission is threaded all the way through accountabilities, it becomes apparent that some of the objectives, strategies, or how you are organized will not get the mission accomplished. When this happens, objectives, strategies, and organizing should be re-thought and checked for alignment with the mission. This is the essence of the iterative strategic thinking process. A cooperatively competent leader is a good iterative strategic thinker. If the linkage between the mission of the enterprise and one's work cannot be drawn, getting others to cooperate in the work will be very difficult.

The second question a competent leader who is strategically thinking must consider is, "Why do we do what we do?" The answer to this "why" question yields the vision of the enterprise. Why did we do what we do at Avascend? Ultimately, we knew we wanted to impact someone's life in a positive way when they really needed it; at a hospital. The words we chose to illustrate our vision, or why we did what we do were, "We do what we do to leave a legacy of faith, hope, and love with everyone we touch." Based upon this vision, is our work simply about parking cars, greeting people, providing directions, shuttling patients and employees, managing parking assets, or collecting parking revenues? On the surface, these are the types of services we offered. By choosing to define our mission and vision this way, we placed a whole new challenge and a higher bar to achieve for our employees. Do you think this might influence the activities and behaviors of our employees who work to serve people at hospitals? Most of our competitors describe themselves as parking or managed contract companies. What might their vision be? You can begin to see how important the vision is in differentiating one company from another. The words you choose to clarify your vision are equally important. Choose them carefully as 'zoomers' are watching.

An enterprise's vision is sometimes described as a purpose statement. The vision should, in fact, help create purpose in those engaged in the work.

When others can answer 'why' they do the work they do, they can commit more deeply to the work. More commitment evidences more cooperation.

The third question a competent leader must ask is, "In what environment will we work to accomplish our mission?" The answer to this question helps clarify the culture of the enterprise. Culture can be defined as the invisible, unspoken, and unwritten norms that govern behavior. Culture in a company focused on optimizing cooperation is normally very different from a company which is not. One significant way to enhance cooperation is to make the culture more visible, less unspoken, and less unwritten. In this way, people know more about the environment in which work is to occur and can choose to engage in or participate in the culture. When culture is invisible, unspoken, and unwritten, people are more likely to bring their own cultural baggage into an enterprise. One person might bring the belief that you can't speak the truth about something unpopular or controversial without negative consequences because, at his or her previous employer, doing so meant you were earmarked as a rebel and put on an exit path. Perhaps the culture preferred in your enterprise is one of truth-telling. Unless you clarify your culture, it is highly unlikely that people will abandon their own norms. Worse yet, some employees will try to impose their norms on your enterprise. This can seriously impair cooperation.

"Culture can be defined as the invisible, unspoken, and unwritten norms that govern behavior."

One way to clarify and illuminate the culture in your enterprise is to survey your leadership and employees about culture. When surveying, there are two questions you should ask: 1) In what culture would you prefer to work? and 2) How have you experienced the culture in this enterprise? Prior to the survey, a team of stakeholders should list a variety of paired descriptors of potential norms that govern behavior. Here are a few examples:

Trusting	vs.	Controlling
Speak first	vs.	Listen first
Don't fix it	vs.	Fix it anyway
Decide fast	vs.	Decide slow
Clear expectations	vs.	Ambiguous expectations
Closed	vs.	Open

The team of stakeholders should determine the type of culture or norms that govern behavior desired in your enterprise. Circle one word-pair or phrase in each row. Discuss what the word or phrase means in its application in your enterprise. The word "trusting" may mean something very different to different people. Come to a consensus on the definition of each cultural word or phrase. Does "trusting" mean permission is not normally required? Does it mean we will always give the benefit of a doubt to a peer and employee without questioning motives? Does it mean we will let someone fail in order to learn? Does it mean we will turn a blind eye to someone even though they have proven time and time again that they cannot be trusted? Are you beginning to see how a lack of clear behavioral norms can impact cooperation? Imagine if these questions go unanswered and are left to the whims and biases of any employee! Once you have done this hard work, don't publish the results. We want the survey responses to be objective.

Now, survey your team with the same word pairs or phrases, asking them both of the previous questions. You may be surprised by the results! Where a significant difference exists between what the team of stakeholders decided was the desired culture and the preferred culture of a respondent, there may be a real lack of fit for the respondent in your enterprise. In this case, the culture preferred by an employee is significantly different than that defined by the leaders of the enterprise. In other words, where trust is part of the enterprise culture, the employee might prefer a culture of control. Whether the leaders of the enterprise want to "fix it anyway", an employee would rather not mess with what is not broken. This should concern leaders greatly and it is better to know now than later!

Where a gap is identified between the stakeholder's culture and how one experiences the enterprise culture, there is leadership work to do. This work will likely include clarifying the culture even more, setting behavioral expectations aligned with the particular norm desired, coaching leaders on how to behave consistent with the culture, and holding leaders accountable for that behavior.

Having a clear and well defined mission, vision, and culture will help set the stage for optimizing cooperation. Anyone who has ever done this work knows it's hard. Words matter. Choose your words carefully and clarify their meaning. You will find this work most beneficial when you attempt to do the second thing cooperatively competent leaders do.

Create a Sense of Purpose

The second thing a cooperatively competent leader does is he or she **creates a sense of purpose.** This is where the hard work done while strategically thinking comes into play. If the mission, vision, and culture are not clear, creating a sense of purpose in others is made exponentially more difficult. Without clarity there is no foundation from and to which to connect others. Confusion will likely cause others to commit less and, consequently, to cooperate less, impairing results.

Purpose is not something given from one to another. Purpose is created in others. You can give someone a job, but you can't directly give them a purpose. Purpose is born in another when a leader takes the what, why, and how of enterprise work and gives it life and meaning. The what, why, and how of enterprise work we just learned are generated through strategic thinking, the first thing a cooperatively competent leader does. They equate to the mission, vision, and culture of the enterprise. But getting these three things written down does nothing to optimize cooperation in and of themselves. We have all seen bronze plaques in the corridors of enterprises that reverently display the mission and vision of the enterprise. Some will even display core values that hint at the culture. In and of themselves, these attractive displays do nothing to get others to cooperate. On the contrary, where these displays are nothing more than displays, the mission, vision, and values or culture of an enterprise are irrelevant to others. Cooperation is likely lacking because a leader hasn't yet taken hold of them and made them real and tangible for others.

"Purpose is born in another when a leader takes the what, why, and how of enterprise work and gives it life and meaning."

Life and meaning born out of the what, why, and how of enterprise work is what creates purpose in another. A cooperatively competent leader must first believe in the mission, vision, and culture, and must be skilled at translating and integrating a person's job or accountabilities into the picture of success. Belief in the mission, vision, and culture of an enterprise is not semantics. People can say they believe in anything, but their behaviors more closely evidence their true beliefs. 'Zoomers' seem to have this sixth sense about what people really believe. Actually, 'zoomers' simply have a hypersensitivity to "fake;" born out of the lack of substance evident in institutions. If you say you believe in the mission and vision, your behavior had better evidence that belief, otherwise, in today's world of post-modern thinkers, you will likely have no one joining you in the work. Fake has no future. Integrity is valued greatly in true leaders and, unfortunately, it is getting harder to find. The leader who remains integral to, not separate and apart from the mission, vision, and culture of the enterprise, has a shot at optimizing cooperation. Others do not.

"Fake has no future."

A cooperatively competent leader must be able to share word pictures or stories of how contributions of a few evidence achieving the mission and lead the enterprise toward achieving its vision. This activity is commonly referred to as vision casting. The behavior is no different than in any other context of someone trying to inspire others. But the application in the context of leadership as we understand it and define it is directly related to getting others to cooperate fully and willingly in the work at hand. If you cannot use your verbal communication, writing, and interpersonal skills to transform the mission, vision, and culture of your enterprise into life and meaning for someone else, it is not likely you will be an effective leader. The purpose created in another when a leader does this work well is a competitive advantage few can duplicate and many wish to emulate.

At Avascend, the healthcare hospitality company I led as CEO, we would regularly hear stories of our employees who, somewhere in the country, performed spontaneous and extraordinary acts of service at a hospital. Families would write us and thank us. Surviving spouses would thank us for the exemplary care and concern we showed them during their many visits to the hospital. We've had employees attend funerals of patients and guests with whom they interacted. One of our employees was named Employee of the Year at a client hospital. He was our employee! We had another promoted to Director of Customer Care, by our client. He was our Manager! We didn't promote him. The client did! Every time we heard a story, it made it to our website. In our training room, copies of letters dominated some large frames where we had memorialized some of the stories about our employees.

Every month at Avascend, we would bring managers from around the country in for training so that we could pour into them our DNA. Do you remember Avascend's mission: to provide service that defies explanation? Each of these weeks, we wanted to put skin on that mission and our vision of leaving a legacy of faith, hope, and love with everyone we touch. The very first morning of the very first day of each week of training, our executive team shined the shoes of our managers. Nothing said; only action. Humbling? Yes. Service that was difficult to explain and justify? Yes. Story for the ages and the employees back at the hospital? Absolutely. More committed managers to our mission? No doubt. Do you see how a leader must own and translate mission, vision, and culture into something real for employees?

Prior to Avascend, I led an enterprise specializing in screen-printing and embroidery of apparel and accessories, named Impact Design. We had over 350 employees working 24 hours-a-day, 5 days-a-week. Impact Design is unique. It happens to be the largest prison industry in one prison facility in the nation. Yes, I said prison. The business operated out of the State of Kansas' largest prison in Lansing, Kansas. At Impact Design, we too had to create a sense of purpose for the employees. In a prison, we certainly could have used other means to get work done, then again, that wouldn't be true leadership now would it? Because we were decorating apparel to display someone's affinity for something, we wanted all our employees (inmates) to focus on sewing and printing someone else's name well. The common phrase we used to help illustrate and create purpose in these men was, "No name says your name like our name."

Mind you, these are inmates, whose names have been in the papers and on the news associated with horrendous activities and crimes. But now . . . their names, though never published, were being associated with something of value to someone else. Can you imagine the feeling and commitment each of these workers had to the enterprise and the work at hand? Each and every day, they knew, because we made sure they knew, that the work they did mattered and that people all over the country were wearing what they produced with pride. What an extraordinary experience in leadership and purposing others! Every enterprise can have a unique purpose like this if only the leader will do the hard work of leading!

I have heard people say often that today's workers work just for a pay check. Might it be that a pay check is all we give them to work for? I would guess that often it is all we give them; no life or meaning in the work. A cooperatively competent leader knows how important creating a sense of purpose in the work is in the art of optimizing cooperation. Little is more important. Creating a sense of purpose has a direct impact on optimizing cooperation. 'Zoomers' thrive on this purpose.

Secure Essential Resources

A cooperatively competent leader will excel at **securing essential resources** for his or her team. A cooperatively competent leader knows that he or she is expected to be the champion for his or her people. A combination of necessity and expectations of the people make this particular facet of leadership a necessity. When someone is invited to join in the work at hand and is expected to fully and willingly commit to the work and do the work, how can the leader expect that same person to secure all the resources he or she needs to do the job? Your people are busy doing the work! It is the leader's role to supply the people with all the things they need. That does not mean they are to withhold things the people need until they ask for it or need it, but it means they are to plan and secure resources enough to insure that the resources are not an obstacle to your employees being successful. Resources might include tools, processes, facilities, equipment, capital, or other workers. Try getting people to cooperate with you in the work and withhold, whether intentionally or by accident, the means with which to accomplish results. How long do you think people will remain fully and willingly committed to the work? My guess and my experience tell me not long.

This makes intuitive sense to many, but it is not as simple as it may look on the surface. Additionally, wanting to be the champion of your people does not make one a leader. Successfully securing resources does. Remember, results matter! Would you be more prone to follow someone who says they will get you a needed resource and doesn't do it, or would you more likely to follow someone who says it and then does it? Determining what resource is needed, when, in what amount and what cost is not always simple. It takes planning and analysis. Every enterprise on the planet must work with limited resources. Your ability as a leader to offer both quantitative and qualitative valuations on options and suggest the best-fit answer and return on the investment will likely determine your success at securing resources. Recognizing and executing this role, knowing that your success will make the difference to those engaged in the work, will determine your cooperative competency©.

Often this means presenting the resources needed to further the enterprise to other leaders in the enterprise or to a Board. Again, speaking and writing skills are essential while tending to this role of a leader. Throw in analytical skills with which to quantify costs and returns, both hard and soft, and this leadership work quickly becomes substantial and time consuming.

"Would you be more prone to follow someone who says they will get you a needed resource and doesn't do it, or would you more likely follow someone who says it and then does it?"

Often, resources needed come in the form of obstacles to remove. Sometimes those committed to the work encounter someone or something that is hindering progress. It can be someone else's boss, a maintenance problem, or even a team member who is not pulling his or her load. Each of these requires knowledge enough or metrics enough to know when an obstacle is hit and the fortitude to intervene and resolve it well, while optimizing cooperation. This doesn't sound so easy.

If the obstacle is a maintenance problem, a strong vendor relationship and a paid-up maintenance contract will aid in quickly resolving the issue. If neither of these two things exists, then your diplomatic skills may well determine the outcome. Neglecting vendor relationships is not a good recipe for optimizing results as your failure to remove a maintenance obstacle will cause others to doubt your ability to champion their needs and they will likely cooperate less. The old days of sellers and buyers sitting on opposite sides of the table are long gone in this post-modern world. Always sit on the same side of the table and negotiate transactions that are mutually beneficial. Fighting against a culture in many enterprises where this is not normal will require talent and perseverance.

If the obstacle is someone else's boss, diplomatic skills will undoubtedly be necessary to intervene productively. The other boss may be working at his or her own common end, not that of the enterprise. Since we know an individual common end leads to a competitive behavior dynamic, a cooperatively competent leader can begin discussions around the enterprise common end. Competing common ends at the enterprise level is a leadership problem. The other boss may be interfering because of unclear accountabilities. He or she may think the area in which he or she is delving is an area for which they have been assigned accountability. This should be able to be clarified by reviewing position descriptions and reviewing accountabilities. Mixed or unclear accountabilities are also a leadership problem. It's possible someone else's boss may be simply trying to throw a wrench into the works of another department. Stranger things have happened! Your prompt, courageous, level-headed, analytical, enterprise-first approach will make the difference in resolving this obstacle efficiently and effectively. Remember, the people who expect you to be their champion, are watching! Get it done and get it done well.

What if the obstacle confronted is a team member? Now the complication and consequences get even greater. There are potential multiple layers of problems if the obstacle is a team member. First of all, did your metrics help indicate a potential problem? How did you find out that the team member was an obstacle? Did your culture help bring the team member obstacle to your attention? You can see that the problem could relate to the culture, a poor communication channel, or a poor metric, in addition to the team member being an obstacle. You may have to fix all four!

Do you have any idea how much time is spent in enterprises trying to figure out what is broken or where obstacles exist? We get management report after management report to help us find out. We audit processes. We observe, looking for an obstacle. Can you imagine what resources would be freed up if you could create a culture where talking freely about obstacles or shortcomings was the norm? All those resources could be redeployed to more productive activities. This kind of culture, to the extent it can be created, would certainly improve cooperation and results.

A team member obstacle is more complicated because the audience for the resolution is large, usually most of the affected team, and the team member is usually known, making objectivity a bit more difficult. The large audience makes not handling a team member obstacle well especially risky as the negative effect on cooperation can be exponential. On the other hand, handling this situation well will exponentially enhance cooperation. There is little debate that knowing someone makes intervention and resolution more difficult, though, far from impossible. A cooperatively competent leader will readily identify the benefit of removing the obstacle to cooperation and will leverage this benefit to overcome any personal qualms about intervening and resolving it productively.

A good place to start before confronting a team member obstacle is to get the facts. What has he or she done or not done? How do we know? Has anyone brought his or her performance and related concerns to his or her attention? Many times you will find that the accused team member has yet to be confronted with any issues. This, too, is a leadership problem. Someone charged with optimizing cooperation must confront problems promptly and effectively. Once the facts support the existence of a team member obstacle, the facts need to be shared with the offending team member. This information should rarely come as a surprise to the team member. You will most assuredly come to one of three reasons for the obstacle; an employee who doesn't want to commit to the work, an employee who can't do the work, or systems and processes that need to be enhanced. These three reasons are discussed at length later in this chapter when we explore a model for solving problems and holding others accountable that aligns perfectly with the goal of optimizing cooperation.

Whether securing resources or removing obstacles, it is incumbent of a cooperatively competent leader to be the champion of the people he or she serves. 'Zoomers' expect it.

Define Communication Channels

Cooperatively competent leaders will be effective at **defining communication channels**. Once people engaged in the work find purpose in it and have the resources they need to be successful, it is now time for the leader to insure that the people working together are talking with one another at the right time about the right stuff to be successful. Rarely do people engaged in work do their job independent of one another. We call the connection points between people who need to communicate "communication channels."

In an effective enterprise, communication channels are cross-functional in nature. Some leaders mistake organization charts for communication channels. Organization charts do not illustrate communication channels. They illustrate decision making authority. In most organization charts, if they did represent communication channels, communication would be expected to go up the chart within a function and over to another function which is too inefficient in today's competitive marketplace. Some enterprises have reorganized horizontally, across different functions, in order for communication channels to more naturally match decision making authority. This is a very effective way to reinforce more natural communication channels within decision making authority. To do this, functional experts must be better leaders as he or she must be able to understand the work across multiple functions, creating purpose and securing resources in areas where he or she may not be particularly technically competent.

In order to design and implement effective communication channels, a cooperatively competent leader must be able to understand the work required, and be able to remove himself or herself from the work in order to watch it function with an eye for communications that are either working or not working. This takes practice. Many leaders make the mistake of identifying a communication failure and believe they fix the problem by delivering the communication to the designated party. Actually, a leader doing this addresses only the symptom. The real problem is a broken communication channel. Fix the channel; fix the problem.

A cooperatively competent leader will ask, "Why did the necessary communication not get to the right person at the right time?" Is it because the people involved don't know what the proper channel is? Could it be because the people involved chose not to comply with the channel? Maybe it's because the leader has never designed an effective channel. Without a well designed, well trained, and monitored channel, cooperation among workers will be difficult and results will not be optimized. The leader must be skilled at each of these activities in order to execute this fourth accountability of a cooperatively competent leader.

Communication channels, when designed well and enforced, help preserve cooperation. For instance, in many enterprises, someone having a bad experience at work is not confronted when he or she shares the experience with others who can do nothing about the experience. That person may be sharing the poor experience with his or her coworkers or another supervisor or boss who is not involved in nor has any accountability for the specific environment in which the experience occurred, spreading ill will. If cooperation is the ultimate goal, then behavior like this, that damages cooperation, must be confronted.

In the enterprises I have led, I have made the following channel a priority. “If you, an employee, are dissatisfied with an experience you have had, you have two approved communication channels: you can elect to talk about it with the person accountable for the experience, or you can talk about it with his or her boss; no one else. Talking with someone else about a negative experience is not acceptable, does not work toward someone else’s success, and violates our desire to optimize cooperation. Consequently, behavior like this will not be tolerated.” In this way, water cooler talk that can easily escalate into a wholesale assault on the cooperation of an enterprise can be eradicated.

Once this type of definition and direction are issued from the leader, the ground is laid for intervention and correction. Outlawing contrary behavior shines a very bright light on behaviors that hurt and hinder cooperation. You will be amazed at how healthy a culture can become if the leader truly honors this channel and intervenes productively. So many times, unbridled communication channels used for communicating poor experiences allow people to spread mistruths. This can often result in extraordinary amounts of a leader’s time chasing down false claims, trying to manage relationships between people, ultimately, keeping leaders and managers from focusing on results. This type of communication channel definition and direction filters out bad and false information, allowing leaders to focus on truth only and optimize cooperation.

"Communication channels, when designed well and enforced, help preserve cooperation."

Efficient and effective communication channels have a direct effect on the cooperation within an enterprise. A cooperatively competent leader is an expert at designing, implementing, monitoring, and fixing these communication channels.

Identify and Develop Other Leaders

This last role of a cooperatively competent leader is more about multiplying the lenses of cooperation than immediately and directly effecting cooperation. A cooperatively competent leader will be intentional about **identifying and developing other leaders**. The understanding and definition of leadership as the art of optimizing cooperation gives every leader a platform from which to develop other leaders.

My experience tells me that leaders are born then made. Some people believe leaders are born only. Certainly, there exists a set of characteristics and traits that lend themselves more easily to leadership. Tendency to take risks, intuitive thinking, and confidence to speak one's mind are some of those traits. People without these traits, though, can exercise these muscles and learn to lead, especially if they understand the nature of and definition of leadership as we do.

"The understanding and definition of leadership as the art of optimizing cooperation gives every leader a platform from which to develop other leaders."

Some enterprises use personality-type indicators like Meyers-Briggs to help identify potential leaders. Others look for observable behaviors that evidence a willingness and capability to lead. Both can be effective. I have had success using the Keirsey Temperament Survey. While the basis of the survey uses the Meyers-Briggs scoring key, Keirsey developed a theory that breaks personality into two fundamental components: one is temperament and the other is character. Temperament is a hard-wiring. It doesn't change when someone is under stress. Character is one's temperament tempered by the Fenvironment in which we find ourselves. To some extent, we can all change based upon the environment in which we work. I have found that temperament is a very good indicator of one's ability to lead as leadership is stressful. When under stress, most people revert to their hard-wiring. Posturing stops.

Keirsey identified four temperament categories in which most people fall. People are identified as either abstract or concrete in their thinking and cooperative or utilitarian in their use of tools. Those identified as abstract thinkers are much more likely to embrace leading others, whether cooperative or utilitarian in their use of tools. The % of people in these categories is around 10% which speaks to the rarity of those wired to lead. Others can learn to lead, but their tendency to need to have experienced something before understanding it limits their ability to adjust to new circumstances. Additionally, those concrete cooperators or guardians don't like change and tend to preserve existing systems. Those concrete utilitarians or artisans find it difficult to work with others as they can be emotional and erratic. Understanding other people's temperament can help identify others as a candidate for leadership.

Whether you use a survey tool or simply observe behaviors, it is necessary that every enterprise identify and invest in other leaders. The investment in leaders can take many shapes and forms. The key is to have an understanding of leadership that allows others to think in different ways. Without this difference in thinking patterns or paradigms, it is unlikely that behaviors will change, leadership will not be learned, and results will not be optimized.

In summary, a cooperatively competent leader does the following five things very well:

- He or she can **strategically think.**
- He or she can **create a sense of purpose.**
- He or she can **secure essential resources.**
- He or she can **define communication channels.**
- He or she can **identify and develop other leaders.**

If you were to ask yourself how many hours a week you spend doing these five things, what would your answer be? Most of my work as an executive leader is spent doing this work which is time consuming and hard. Increasing your cooperative competency© is hard work, but the dividends in the form of enhanced cooperation and, ultimately, optimized results are worth every moment of practice and application.

Hold Others Accountable While Optimizing Cooperation

Those of you who still think defining leadership as optimizing cooperation is "soft," take heart. Here is where accountability comes into play. This model is fully aligned with optimizing cooperation and doubles as a great problem solving model. How a lack of results is handled makes a huge difference, both from a cooperative perspective and a fix-the-problem perspective. The model starts with the leader monitoring results. The cooperatively competent leader is best served by entering this model with a belief that employees, those engaged in the work, both want to and can do the work. This belief is essential to optimizing cooperation, and it is true in my experience. In the language made mainstream by Jim Collins in his book, *Good to Great*, believe that the right people are on the bus and that they are in the right seat on the bus until you determine otherwise. Presuming otherwise, may cause you as a leader to prematurely judge a circumstance and levy consequences that will damage cooperation. This must be avoided at all costs.

If you struggle with this belief, consider the alternatives. You can presume that people don't want to do the work. How would you behave with this paradigm? As a leader believing this, you would likely feel like you had to "stay on top of your workers," insure that they constantly know that you are the boss, and that there are serious consequences for either not doing what you wanted them to do, or for doing something that you did not ask of them. Does this sound like you?

You can also presume that people can't do the work. I would imagine believing this would cause you to constantly either check someone's work or do the work for them. How would that work for you? If you were to presume both of these thoughts; that workers neither want to nor can do the work, you would likely never make it to or be blind to the set of problems that you cause! I dare say that people working for you would rarely commit to the work and your results would be fair at best. Don't go there! People want to do something meaningful at work and most people are plenty talented to do it. Believe it!

Now, back to the model . . . When a negative symptom or result occurs, the cooperatively competent leader will work through the model below:

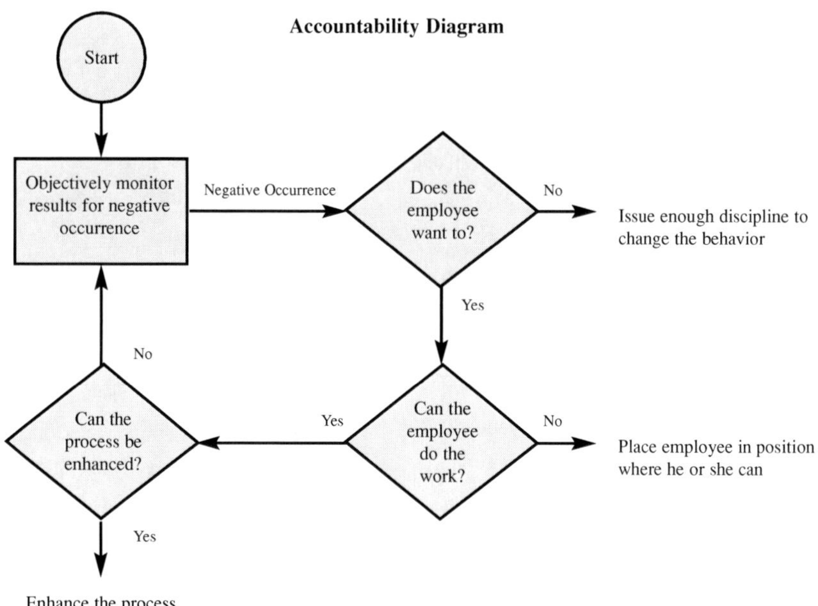

The first question a cooperatively competent leader will ask is, "Did the employee involved want to do the work?" The answer to this question will indicate the level of the employee's willingness to do the work. At the point your answer to this question is, "no," then enough discipline should be issued to change the behavior. Sometimes a simple discussion will do. I remember discussing the poor performance of an employee for whom I was responsible. I was prepared to document the conversation, but I could tell she wanted to do the work just through our conversation. Because of our discussion and her observable reaction to that discussion, I threw the paper in the trash right in front of her as a covenant of trust in her and her commitment to do better. Guess what? She never violated that trust.

At other times, a warning, suspension, or even termination will be the consequence. A mismatch between the negative result, the employee's unwillingness, and the discipline can seriously effect cooperation. **Remember, issue only enough discipline to change the behavior.** You are trying to gain the willingness and commitment of the employee. They may be competent at the work, but if they don't want to commit to the work or enterprise, tolerating their mediocre commitment by issuing too little discipline will breed mediocrity. Issuing no discipline will certainly send a message of tolerance to those who don't care. Want to irreparably damage cooperation? Keep competent people who don't want to commit and cooperate. Many enterprises do this believing they can't afford to lose a high performing individual, yet they set the stage for their enterprise's demise because they place cooperation second to individual performance. Issuing discipline in excess of that needed to change behavior will result in anger and frustration, causing diminished cooperation and time spent solving cooperative problems. If the answer to the first question, "Did the employee involved want to do the work?" is "yes," go to the second question.

"Want to irreparably damage cooperation? Keep competent people who don't want to commit and cooperate."

The second question a cooperatively competent leader will ask is, "Can the employee involved do the work?" This is a question of one's capability. At the point your answer to this question is, "no," then the enterprise is best served by finding other role in the enterprise where the incapable employee can be successful. If no place exists, then separation may be the only option. Retaining the employee who is incapable is important if you can, because their full commitment has already been tested by answering question #1, "yes." I've seen people who have been promoted to management who simply could not adjust to the work or role. In many cases, we moved them back to a position that fit their skill set, preserving their job, leveraging their commitment to the work, and optimizing cooperation. What if you were to leave the incapable person in place? Results would suffer, mediocrity would be the message, and, to the extent leaders would continue to talk about results, integrity would be lost. Why else might others say the person is left in place if they are incapable? He or she must know someone? Perhaps the leader plays favorites? Maybe results are not really as important as first believed. You can bet 'zoomers' have these things on their radars! What happens if you discipline an employee who can't do the work? Imagine whipping a horse you were riding that was running as fast as it could go? Do you think the horse might get angry? So does the employee. None of these consequences will optimize cooperation. If the answer to the second question, "Can the employee involved do the work?" is "yes," go on to the third question.

If an employee wants to and can do the work, which is most often the case, then there is only one other option that may cause the negative symptom or result. The third question is, "Can the system or process be enhanced?" Those of you who have studied W. Edwards Deming will find this next step familiar. Deming coached that minimizing or eliminating variation in the process is the way to improve quality. This part of the model is similar. If the only variable left to address is the process, investigate if it can be enhanced. This question will sometimes lead to enhancing training or closing a loop hole in an existing process. In my experience, most problem solving and accountability actions will be done in this part of the model. Where an employee is part of the core problem, accountability will be enforced. Where process variation is the problem, which is likely the case because most employees want to and can do the work, problem solving will result in corrective action, preventing a repeat of the negative symptom or result.

In a few situations a leader will make it all the way around the model without identifying the core problem. In this case there is no identifiable cause of the negative symptom or result. Keep monitoring results and follow the model when a negative symptom or result occurs again. Complying with this model for holding others accountable and problem solving will insure that cooperation is always optimized.

I have found one other benefit when using this model. At Avascend, where we specialized in hospitality, holding others accountable was difficult because hospitality people like to be nice. **Sometimes they are too nice**, avoiding the interactions that come with holding others accountable. This phenomenon is definitely mirrored in most churches and other enterprises where owners just want everyone to be happy. This model provides a way that nice people can hold others accountable. It takes away the fear of intervening and having to use discipline where discipline is not required, while placing an emphasis on fixing processes. This model also preserves relationships, regardless of the consequence. An employee disciplined severely has made it clear that they choose not to commit to the work. An employee moved to a place where he or she can be successful is usually grateful and appreciative, though disappointed. All employees involved in processes that are refined and most often produce excellent results are more productive. No matter the consequence, following this model will optimize cooperation and, ultimately, optimize results.

OTHER CONTEMPORARY THINKING

KEN BLANCHARD

The One Minute Manager, co-authored by Ken Blanchard is an iconic book about how to lead people. Though it was published decades ago as one of the first "fable-type" business books; easy to read and built around a fictitious story; it remains a best seller and relevant today.

I consider *The One Minute Manager* one of the best books for illustrating accountability. Accountability starts with clarity. Accountability is not possible without the clarity of an objective or goal. Blanchard's **one minute goal setting** is a great illustration of where accountability starts. I use a real sword to help executives remember the importance of one-minute goal setting. Often, I will ask a volunteer to show us how they would use the sword if they were conveying a goal to others. Invariably, they hold the sword up and pointed forward, as if charging the hill and clarifying the goal.

A goal is nothing if results are not monitored and while monitoring, managers are going see some people doing the right things. This is where a **one minute praising** is important. To create an object lesson for executives, I ask a volunteer to show how they would use the sword to offer a one-minute praising. If they are familiar at all with medieval movies, they know that placing the sword on the shoulder of one being knighted, alternating between shoulders, is the sign of knighthood and a praising. Usually, pleasing smiles and giggles fill the room after this object lesson.

Also, while monitoring, leaders are bound to see some things that are not right. When we begin down this path, the tenor in the room usually changes. Finally, we get to what Blanchard calls a **one minute reprimand**. At the mention of the word, the room begins to fill with nervous chuckles as the executives can see what is coming with the sword. I, again, ask a volunteer to show us how the sword might be used to illustrate a one minute reprimand. Intuitively, they either stab at an invisible person in front of them or they move the sword horizontally across what is logically the region of the neck of another. Of course, the room laughs heartily. I respond with a firm, "No." Silence follows.

I then take the sword from the volunteer, ask them if they trust me, and illustrate that the first thing a leader does before issuing a one minute reprimand is to figuratively, hand the sword to the person receiving the reprimand. In this way, the recipient knows the reprimand is not personal and they know you are not there to kill them. They know you have the sword. If you want to improve that person's performance, don't pull it out! Now have a conversation about the behavior that needs to change. Agree on behaviors going forward and discuss future consequences and the level of trust between you two for the future behaviors. Figuratively, take the sword back, re-sheath it, and continue. This illustration is one that usually hits home with executives. Reprimands don't have to be difficult, but they are essential. This illustration often helps managers and executives who are too nice deal with issues of accountability.

Thanks to Ken Blanchard, these one-minute gems are still relevant and critical to a leader's ability to optimize cooperation. If you haven't read this book recently, re-read it. It's still a best seller, and rightly so.

RESULTS MATTER

The phrase "results matter" seems so simple and so intuitive in an enterprise! Yet, when having to choose between results and a relationship with someone, many people choose to preserve a relationship over achieve results. Certainly, many people who have been promoted beyond their level of competence spend a great deal of time protecting their status, most often at the expense of results. If these decisions and activities are being made in the context of an enterprise, a future battle for optimal results is looming. Working relationships forged for any purpose other than optimizing results, whether the relationship is intended to be personal or formed to protect oneself, will work counter to optimizing results. Can relationships and optimizing results coexist? They must and they can, but in an enterprise, relationships based upon any criteria other than working together toward a common end will render less-than-optimal results.

'Zoomers' pose an especially unique problem with working relationships. Many 'zoomers' have been conditioned to be 'lone wolves.' They exist for themselves, live in their own worlds, and relate through impersonal and potentially distorted means using one of many social networking tools. Face-to-face, many don't know how to behave. Writing and talking skills are secondary to key-boarding or "thumbing" text messages. This isolated and distorted world is comfortable for many 'zoomers,' though unhealthy. They are suspect of any place where they might be exploited or forced to conform to the institutional status quo.

A huge challenge for 21st Century enterprise leaders is creating a culture where 'zoomers' feel free to express themselves and learn behaviors critical to team work and cooperation. Much like heat and pressure causes iron-ons to stick to fabric, heat and pressure can be used to remove them. The same type of inverted process holds true for 'zoomer' relationships. Their withdrawal from honest interpersonal relationships, forged through doubt in institutions lacking substance, not the least of which they were exposed to in their own home watching the institution of marriage unravel before their very eyes, can be reversed by honest, integral, transparent, and forthright engagement in something bigger than themselves. They have seen this so rarely that the leader who can successfully convince 'zoomers' that working together can produce great results and something bigger than any one person can produce, will have a significant competitive advantage.

Results are the desired outcome of any effort, whether by an individual or by a team of people. The bottom line is that, regardless of the effort, results matter. If you're an executive or a leader of a subset of an enterprise, you know that the outcomes for which you are responsible are important. Many executives erroneously believe that the only people who care about results and outcomes are the shareholders and owners. Is this true? This certainly becomes a self-fulfilling prophecy if the leader's behavior mirrors this belief. Here is what I mean. Executives and leaders who believe this, often behave in ways that cause others to care **less** about results. If someone is viewed as not caring about results, is information shared? Are expectations made clear or are they skimmed over believing that the employee only responds to supervision and monitoring? Are people released to perform or is strict monitoring the only way to squeeze performance out of folks? Are people trusted with company resources or are control processes so cumbersome that people just give up pursuing them because of all the red tape?

In every enterprise, there are many stakeholders who care deeply about results, if only the leader will engage and release them in pursuit thereof. Every employee, vendor, and customer is a stakeholder in the enterprise with a vested interest in success, and success is a product of achieving desired results. Failure to accept and practice this belief will debilitate 'zoomers,' damage cooperation, and produce lackluster results.

There are two sets of behavioral dynamics that govern most relationships, whether within the enterprise, or otherwise. Understanding these and being consciously competent in handling different environments will help you lead more effectively toward optimal results. One set is aimed at the common good and the other set is aimed at the common end. Common good behavioral dynamics do not produce optimal results. A social relationship is one example where common good behavioral dynamics govern. In a social relationship, results don't matter at all. Socially, you and another person are together simply to enjoy one another's company. You will find this dynamic governing outside of work or at a social function.

Common good behavioral dynamics also govern in a political relationship. In a political relationship, the parties are primarily concerned with an outcome that is satisfactory to everyone; a compromise, if you will. We hear the word compromise often, especially in arms-length negotiations. If you hear the word compromise within the work of your enterprise, beware! You are about to sub-optimize results! Invest the time and energy to reach consensus, not compromise. Don't fall for the ploy of another to be satisfied with a less-than-optimal resolution without trying to reach consensus. The time and effort, though sometimes frustrating to endure, will generate better results. And certainly don't vote. Someone always losses when a vote is taken and their contrary position is affirmed by losing. Though voting is quick, cooperation can be seriously damaged when a vote is taken. If faced with a deadline, a necessary decision, and time has run out, the leader should make the decision and begin performing damage control in order to mitigate damage from a lack of consensus and to protect cooperation.

Contrary to common good behavioral dynamics, common end dynamics have the potential to optimize results. One relationship where this common end dynamic governs is in a competitive relationship. A competitive relationship exists where each party brings his or her own common end, not an agreed upon or leader-specified common end. Competitive work environments are created when the leader does not specify a common end, so people come together bringing their own common ends, which often compete. A competitive working relationship does not optimize results.

I learned the truth of this when I began working in the apparel business, where I spent most of career. As just a young pup, I didn't know any better than to watch, learn and follow along with the practice of piece rate incentive compensation for employees performing sewing assembly operations. This practice had long been used in the apparel business. Being a good student, I studied how these work-quickly-and-get-paid-based-upon-your-productivity systems worked. In apparel manufacturing plants, workers were normally paid a varying hourly wage based upon their productivity versus an engineered standard. The quicker you worked with the least amount of wasted motion, the more pay your could earn. It didn't seem so bad at first. I'm all for hard work and reaping the rewards of a job well done.

But what happened to the resulting end product was far from optimal. Because each individual operation was incented to achieve maximum efficiency or each individual operation assumed its own "common end," little or no regard was given to work-in-process or quality. What was saved in direct labor through efficiency was lost in accumulating massive inventories of sub-standard product that had to be inspected. These "competing" ends within a factory served to seriously sub-optimize results. What a visual lesson of varying common ends for me! This is what an enterprise without a leader-specified common end looks like. A term I have heard used to represent this set of circumstances is "thrashing." People, departments, and positions work against one another or not for the whole due to a lack of common end definition.

There is a common thread where competitive relationships exist. Where you find competitive relationships, you will find a lack of leadership. In my apparel industry example, plant managers relied on incentive pay to keep workers working. If they didn't, their pay would go down. This is a case of designing a compensation system that causes others to work in lieu of purposing them as good leaders will do. They didn't exhibit leadership. They exhibited the ability to build a system of monitoring and compensating that caused people to do work consistent with varying common ends.

In the succeeding companies in which I held leadership positions; all of them; after having developed both an expertise in and frustration with piece rate incentive pay systems, we threw the incentive plans out the door, gave hourly wages to the workers and committed ourselves to leading people. You have to trust people in order to make a decision like this. We will discuss the benefit of trusting people, especially 'zoomers,' in a later chapter. This was a much harder road to take, but in all cases we were able to garner the full and willing commitment of the people and each company became more competitive and more difficult to match or overtake in the marketplace.

Most people associate competitive behavioral dynamics with the marketplace. Actually, this kind of relationship exists in almost every kind of enterprise. These competing common ends can also be found in meetings and discussions among peers and associates. How many times have you been in a meeting, listening to various opinions, without any idea what the ultimate outcome is desired from the meeting or discussion? In order to avoid competitive dynamics, the leader must specify a common end. Don't leave common ends to be defined by competing engineered standards or a lack of clarity!

A cooperative relationship is the only relationship in which and through which results are optimized. In these relationships, the leader specifies a common end and the parties commit to achieving it together. The leader casts vision, purposes people, organizes for outcomes, assigns accountabilities and supports his or her people as they work toward the common end that he or she specified, whether in a meeting, discussion, or as part of the business strategy.

"If you hear the word compromise within the work of your enterprise, beware! You are about to sub-optimize results! Invest the time and energy to reach consensus, not compromise."

Results matter. Performance counts. Leadership makes the difference. Let's connect the dots. From the discussion above, results are important to everyone and they are the only reason for relationships in an enterprise. Leadership is the difference maker because it focuses on optimizing cooperation within working relationships, the ultimate goal of an enterprise, because failure to get others to fully and willingly commit to the work will be an enterprise's ultimate obstacle to success. Performance is the link between leadership and results in an enterprise. We can illustrate this relationship like this:

Leadership → Performance → Results

Poor results indicate the need to identify core problems and coach improvement. Can performance be measured? We do it all the time, but its ultimate measure is only through results. If results are not satisfactory, then performance must not be satisfactory. If performance is not satisfactory, then leadership is not satisfactory. Many leaders try to dilute problem solving by whitewashing results to look better than they actually are. This practice only delays the inevitable assessment of performance. Additionally, some leaders unable to whitewash results, invent all sorts of excuses why performance is lacking. The fact is performance is the accountability of the leader.

Checking the alignment of our belief that *leadership is the art of optimizing cooperation* with *leadership makes the difference*, we can intuitively understand that people fully and willingly committed to the work perform better and produce better results. The lesson here is to monitor and judge results and always coach leadership. Leadership makes the difference.

Is it possible to get a false positive in an enterprise where results are satisfactory, but leadership and performance lack? Yes. We mentioned earlier how means like threatening others, withholding things others need, controlling access to tools, and providing an undesirable option for abandoning the effort will cause others to follow and will produce some level of results, at least in the short term. How does an executive protect against the complacency that accompanies satisfactory, yet less than optimal results?

Let's look at a basketball team example to explore this scenario. We have all seen basketball teams that have won a game, but played very poorly. In a successful basketball program that produces perennial champions, what do you hear the coach say after a lack luster performance, yet a win? Do you hear, "A win is a win. I am pleased with our kids for simply winning because that is the result we want. All we seek to do is score more points than the opponent." Or are you more likely to hear, "We played like crap! We have a long way to go to be the type of team we can be, and we will be practicing hard to perform better in our next game." In a championship program, you will hear the latter. Why? Because the leader, the coach, not only monitors results, but he or she keeps a sharp eye and feel for the fundamentals that constantly and consistently produce optimal results.

The same is true of successful leaders. While they monitor results closely, they also keep a sharp eye on the fundamentals that produce results. With leadership making the difference, these fundamentals almost always involve executives coaching the finer points of leadership. To be an effective enterprise leader, it is critical that you be able to, not only lead, but understand leadership in such a way that leadership can be coached, learned, and multiplied in your enterprise. This is one of the greatest advantages of a clear and complete definition of leadership. That is why defining leadership as the art of optimizing cooperation is so important. This fundamental, governing dynamic, allows us as leaders to monitor and coach leadership well.

"To be an effective enterprise leader, it is critical you be able to, not only lead, but understand leadership in such a way that leadership can be coached, learned, and multiplied in your enterprise."

Now that we have a new understanding and belief in leadership, let's understand the basic formula for monitoring results and intervening to coach improved leadership. An executive focused on results that matter and committed to coaching leadership must be able to do three broadly-defined things to optimize cooperation in his or her enterprise.

#1 Recognize where cooperation lacks
#2 Choose to intervene, and
#3 Intervene productively

Each of these has its own set of difficulties.

The first thing an executive leader must do in a broad sense is recognize that something is wrong with cooperation. This infers that the executive must be close enough to notice that something is not right or somehow be notified that something is wrong. If you are someone who generally does not like bad news, then leadership is going to be difficult for you. Better leaders constantly hunt for that which needs to be fixed, improved upon, or eliminated. When cooperation is the goal, there is always something going on that is hurting cooperation. I call things not being right "the stink." It is imperative that an executive be close enough to what is happening to "smell the stink."

An executive practicing leadership as we have defined it, the art of optimizing cooperation, will recognize different attitudes or behaviors as either indicative of cooperation; people working together toward a common result, or indicative of a lack of cooperation; people working at cross purposes toward something other than a common end. Look for these kinds of symptoms that often result in a lack of cooperation.

- Sour dispositions
- Arrogance or selfishness
- Frequent complaints

These symptoms can be subtle and can be disguised very well. An employee who rolls his or her eyes at an announcement may indicate a lack of cooperation. Using the pronoun, "I" all the time can be indicative of selfishness or arrogance and a lack of cooperation. Complaints, as juvenile and as petty as they may be, can indicate poor morale and can be indicative of poor cooperation. When morale is low, everything is a problem. When morale is high, the little things are simply that; little things. Low morale indicates a cooperation problem.

This seems simple, but many executives who view employees as always dissatisfied or complaining will rarely catch these signals. They will write these symptoms off, believing that they are born out of something other than their own behaviors. In some cases dissatisfaction and complaints will be born out of something else, but thinking this way will cause numerous indications of poor cooperation to be missed; making optimizing cooperation nearly impossible. A better executive leader will assume that every one of these symptoms is in response to something within his or her control. How does an executive know what caused the symptom? Ask! If you see someone roll his or her eyes, say, "I saw you roll your eyes. Do you not believe what I am saying? Why don't you believe?" The answer can be both revealing and painful to a leader. Listen well and learn. Remember, recognizing when cooperation is hindered is one of the first steps in competent leadership.

The second broadly-defined thing a competent leader will do well is choose to intervene. Once a cooperative symptom is identified, a competent leader will choose to intervene. This is far from automatic; even for a seasoned leader. There are several reasons for a lack of intervention. First and foremost, any intervention will take time and effort. Many executives claim to be too busy, but if cooperation is the ultimate goal, then failure to intervene could promptly put the cooperation within your enterprise at peril. Second, intervention into attitudes and behaviors that hinder cooperation can involve emotions and can often get into areas where leaders don't often want to go. An employee who is upset about a decision or about the way something was handled, may release his or her frustration on you. Some people simply don't want to endure this. As a competent leader, though, you must in order to get to the bottom of what is causing the lack of cooperation. Choosing to intervene can be a difficult decision, but it is imperative if cooperation is ultimately to be optimized.

It does no good for an executive to intervene, if he or she does not intervene productively. Recognizing and choosing to intervene can backfire if the way you handle the situation produces a lack of cooperation. The best tool to use once you choose to intervene is to ask questions, listen, and respond in a way that consciously promotes cooperation. You may have to make a commitment to change a behavior or change a decision if the employee brings you a legitimate perspective whereby cooperation was hurt. If not, you will likely be placed in a position to explain the "why's" behind a decision. This alone will cause either the employee to accept the decision better, enhancing cooperation, or will help you determine that the values of the employee are misaligned with those of the enterprise. If the latter is true, it is better to part ways because misaligned values can wreak havoc on and seriously damage cooperation.

Results matter to 'zoomers.' Their rebellion isn't against profit. It's against how those profits are used and against the means used to get them. Ultimately, we all know that results will be better when we work together toward something meaningful. 'Zoomers' understand that sometimes intervention is required to correct behavior and cooperation is the best practice. When this cooperation becomes the ultimate goal of an enterprise, and constructive intervention becomes the practice, 'zoomers' engage. At that point, where results matter to 'zoomers,' you have the critical mass to do something extraordinary!

OTHER CONTEMPORARY THINKING

JIM COLLINS

Jim Collins, author of many books including *Good to Great* and *How the Mighty Fall* (both great books), is an objective researcher whose findings have helped many executives conceptualize their enterprise's road to success or their enterprise's adjustment in their trajectory. He began his research for *Good to Great* with the premise that the impact of leadership on enterprise results is arguable.

Let me share with you and remind you where he ended up at the end of these two books. If you recall, Collins introduced the concept of a Level-5 Leader after studying 11 companies who moved from good to great. It was one of the principal findings in the book. Though the concept of leadership he began with was different than that of a Level-5 Leader, he confirmed that a leader like those in the 11 companies was a common factor in their rise to sustained success or greatness. As a review of his findings, the Level-5 Leader has these characteristics:

- They are ambitious for the cause, the organization, and the work **first**, not themselves

- They have a fierce resolve to do whatever it takes to make good on the ambition
- He or she displays an odd blend of personal humility and professional will

He shares, after studying companies that have fallen sharply from success in *How the Mighty Fall*, that while success cannot be attributed solely to a strong leader, the wrong leader in place can bring a company to a very quick and untimely death. He writes, "Truly great organizations prosper through multiple generations of leaders, the exact opposite of being built around a single great leader, great idea, or specific program. Leaders in great organizations build catalytic mechanisms to stimulate progress and do not depend upon having a charismatic personality to get things done; indeed, many have had a "charisma bypass."

Skeptic or not, he validates the impact a leader and his or her leadership can have on an enterprise.

BUILD TRUST

At the core of any effort to preserve or increase cooperation is trust. This is especially true of environments involving post-modern thinkers like the 'zoomers.' Trust is everything. Violate trust; damage cooperation. Enhance trust; optimize cooperation. Since we know that optimizing cooperation is the ultimate goal of an enterprise, then enhancing trust is critical to optimizing results and outcomes. Trust, if lost, is almost impossible to regain in the short or intermediate term, so it is critical to enhance trust with each decision the leader makes.

Institutions have left many scars with people who have committed themselves to the work and been let down by the reality that they are expendable and subject to the whim and fancy of shareholders and owners. This generation is known for having a knack for identifying a fake or fraud earlier than most. Why? Because they are hypersensitive to trust. If they don't trust you, they won't commit. If they do trust you, you can't keep them from committing. In today's marketplace, trust is a critical factor in getting others to fully and willingly commit to the work.

Trust is a two-way street. Not only must leaders be trustworthy, but they must trust others. I survey teams all the time and ask if those present are trustworthy. Rarely has anyone answered the, "Are you trustworthy?" question, "No." Even at Impact Design, in the prison, the inmate employees answered, "Yes!" But answers to the question, "Do you trust others?" are significantly different. Many people don't trust others. Many of us are incapable of trusting others. Our ability to trust has been damaged every time we have been burned after taking the chance to trust someone else. The scars run deep and long, causing pain enough to generate decisions aimed at doing nothing but avoiding that pain. So we choose not to trust.

As a leader, you cannot **not** trust other people and be successful. Below is a model that illustrates why trusting others is so important to leadership. Remember our goal is to optimize cooperation. If a person is not trustworthy and not trusted, you have an environment of **appropriate control**. You can find this type of environment in a prison. Offenders have lost the trust of the public and have been labeled not trustworthy, and they are not trusted; left to the custody, care, and control of the local, state, or federal government. What kind of environment can you expect if you trust others who are not trustworthy? You can expect **damage control**. This can happen in any enterprise and does pose some risk to results and outcomes. Mitigating this potential, though, is that fact that most people are trustworthy, so trusting others ultimately poses minimal risks.

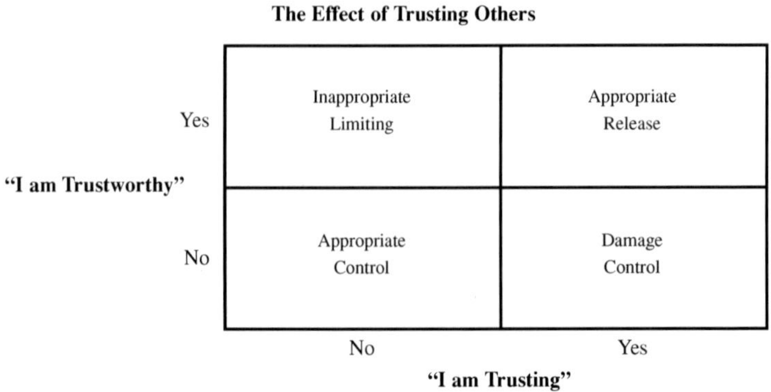

What happens when we don't trust people who are trustworthy? This is where I believe most enterprises are. In this environment, people are not released to perform. They are controlled and limited. This is an **inappropriate limiting** environment. This kind of environment chokes people and leads to despair, frustration, and a lack of commitment. We as leaders must trust those who are trustworthy. This is an **appropriate release** environment. We must do so, even if that means we must take a chance on the few that are not trustworthy. We can control the damage. For the trustworthy people, we can either limit them or release them. Which of these environments do you think breeds more full and willing commitment to the work? Releasing workers optimizes results and fuels trust, an essential ingredient in gaining the cooperation of others.

It is likely your employees have been burned before when they trusted another person, especially a boss. Given this likelihood, it is not enough to simply trust others, but you must consciously build trust. How does a leader build trust?

Early in my career, I assumed the accountability for the manufacturing and operations of a large apparel manufacturing operation. I knew that my predecessor had violated the trust of many employees. More than once I saw what he said and what he did. I could tell trust lacked by the initial adversarial glares and conversations I had with those I was to lead. They weren't going to trust me. Consequently, I made it a critical goal to build and earn their trust. One day in a shift meeting, I wanted help in identifying some productivity initiatives from the employees. I made it a point that the enterprise wants to reward talent and that anyone who can think of and implement productivity improvements is talented. After several minutes of silence, I knew they did not believe me. Their posture and silence told me so. I took another figurative step toward them and stated that I would give a $.50/hour raise immediately to the first person to give me a productivity improvement idea. A young man took a chance and gave me an idea. I thanked him, adjourned the meeting, and immediately went to Human Resources to give him the raise I promised. I had to fight the bureaucracy to get it, but I ultimately persevered. He didn't believe me until he saw the raise on his next check. After seeing the raise I promised, he made it a point to tell everyone, and I mean everyone, that I did what I said I would do. I gained huge trust that day among the employees as someone who does what he says he is going to do.

If you dissect what happened here, it is easy to see how trust was built. I promised something and I delivered it. My brother, who is a psychiatrist, once asked me how someone could become an authority figure. He told me that someone becomes an authority figure by saying something, then doing it. Similarly, becoming trusted or building trust is all about doing what you say. Most people know this, but instead of boldly saying things in order to make big things happen, they say very little or nothing, in order to insure they can deliver everything they say. Does this sound like you? Leaders cannot be afraid to make commitments to secure resources or remove obstacles. While trust may not be lost in a leader due to his or her failure to deliver, certainly confidence in the leader will suffer and cooperation will diminish if they only deliver when the challenge is simple and easy. A strong leader will make relevant, bold promises and deliver on them. In doing so, he or she will build trust.

I learned an important lesson about trust when I took over the apparel manufacturing and operations. I learned that some people don't want to trust or can't trust and they want others to join them in their dissension. As the tide of people began to trust me as the leader, it was obvious that a few people were not coming along. They were constantly challenging decisions and spreading ill-will among the other workers, causing some to doubt whether trust was well-placed in me. After numerous observations, I confronted this pair of employees about whether they could or would trust me. They said they could and would. I sealed our agreement with the expectation that they would only question decisions made with those making the decisions and not other employees. Our agreement lasted a few days until I was made aware that the two were causing unrest again. I called them into my office and unceremoniously fired both of them for violating our agreement. They ultimately sued the company for wrongful discharge but didn't win. Why didn't they win? The company did its job by thoroughly explaining expectations, trusting that the employees would comply, and acting fairly when they violated the agreement. What do you think the response from the rest of the work force was as they observed our agreement and our response? It became widely known that trust was a critical factor in our work culture. People began to understand it is OK to question decisions, but to do so with the right people. Spreading unrest and ill-will will get you fired where cooperation is to be optimized. And quickly!

Trusting others and building trust are critical to optimizing cooperation. Yet many leaders tear trust down, irreparably damaging cooperation. Many do so out of ignorance or out of unconscious incompetence. Here's how. The first choice a leader makes is to carry himself or herself in a particular way. Many people in a position to lead were the best at what they did and have had success all along the way. This success has been reinforced with promotions and salary increases. The confidence that comes with such moves often leads to pride, which can cause a leader to carry himself or herself with an air of **invulnerability**. This is trouble without knowing it yet. See the diagram below and the explanations that follow to understand how this initial decision of a leader can significantly affect results.

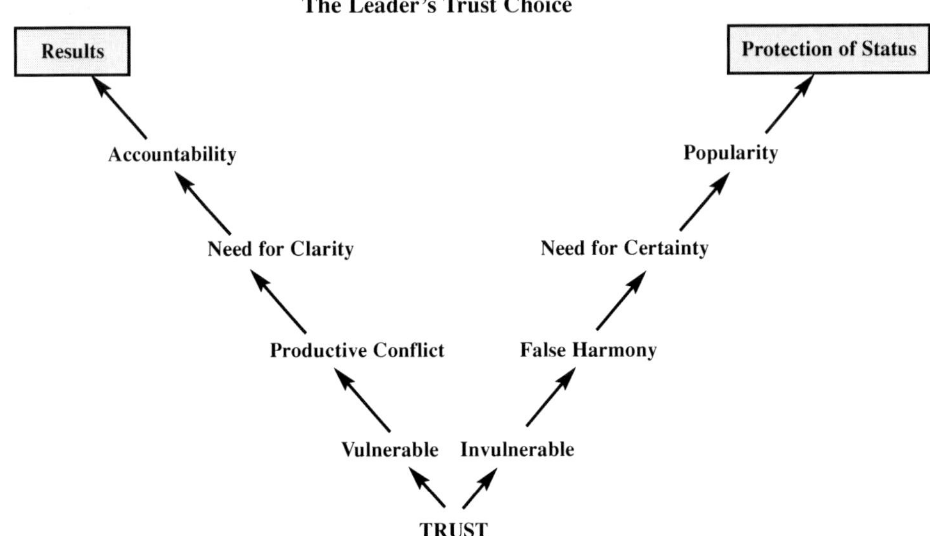

Source: Summary of thoughts from Patrick Lencioni's, *Five Temptations of a CEO*

An invulnerable leader behaves in a way that creates fear in many people. The fear is born out of either the headstrong nature of the leader or out of the lack of listening or lack of admitting fault with followers. This type of, "I am always right," behavior diminishes trust. 'Zoomers' know better. The associated fear will result in a culture of **false harmony**, where to the leader's face, everyone agrees and shakes their heads politely, "yes," whether they agree or not. Fear of the leader creates too much risk if a dissenting opinion is offered. We would call these 'yes men or women.' False harmony leads to a **need for certainty** before any one does any work because the consequence of failing or letting the invulnerable leader down is just too severe or unknown.

Because work is not being done waiting on the leader, **popularity** becomes a viable individual end as people seek the approval of the leader in order to avoid any potential damage to their position. We call this phase **protecting status** and it is exactly where a leader choosing to be invulnerable leads the people in an enterprise. This is all too common and often the result of a leader who behaves like he or she has seen other leaders lead; with an air of invulnerability. Some people even avoid leading others because they do not want to be associated with this type of leadership style, enterprise, or related results.

On the other hand, a leader could choose to carry himself or herself with an air of **vulnerability**. When I say vulnerability, I am not inferring a lack of strength or confidence. I am talking about carrying oneself with an honest and transparent acknowledgment that he or she needs others to help do the work and to cover the blind spots that each of us have in our own strength profile. We are all better at some things than others. Others know it. Why don't we just admit it?! Admitting what others already know builds trust.

A vulnerable leader, visibly transparent and thankful for others with varying talents, will create a culture of **productive conflict**, welcoming other ideas and wisdom from multiple sources. Because people with many perspectives contribute to the cause, enterprises usually reach better solutions and better buy-in from others in this kind of culture. **Clarity** is the only need at this point, not certainty. The leader can clarify and assign the work to others in the enterprise. This clarity allows the leader to hold others accountable and **accountability** breeds **results**. This is the natural end or result of a leader who chooses to carry him or herself with an air of vulnerability. Your enterprise or subset of an enterprise can either achieve results or protection of status based solely on the way you carry yourself. That's a bit humbling, isn't it?! If you want to optimize cooperation and build trust, be vulnerable not invulnerable.

"Admitting what others already know builds trust."

Often when trust is breached or diminished, it is impossible to repair. There is rarely enough time to re-build a relationship where trust is broken. At all the companies I have led I would tell employees often, "If you can be trusted, there is nothing you can do to lose your job. If you can't be trusted, there is nothing you can do to keep it." This placed the ultimate value on trust within the enterprise.

"Seeing" trust is a skill that is learned. In almost every question an employee asks a leader, there is a trust component. Not seeing it can cause a leader to damage trust and cooperation irreparably. A question like, "Why does this work need to be done?" has both a content component and an intent component. For instance, it is possible that the employee really wants to know why the work needs to be done. Perhaps they didn't hear the 'why' in previous conversations. This is the content component. On the other hand, perhaps they did, but aren't sure they can rely on your judgment or advice. This is an intent component. If you answer the question only literally, by telling them why the works needs to be done, you will have missed an important opportunity to build trust, especially if they, in fact, are questioning your judgment or advice. If you send them away as if they are stupid for asking the question, you will most certainly damage trust. If you tell them why, thank them for asking for clarification, and ask them why they don't trust you when the work is requested, you will likely build trust. Seeing this intent is learned and requires seasoned leadership lenses.

Stephen M.R. Covey wrote a great book entitled *The Speed of Trust.* If you have ever doubted the critical importance of trust in an enterprise, read this book! It is outstanding. He provides very practical and logical evidence from his experiences about the effect of trust on an enterprise's success. One of the rational formulas he shares in his book is R = t(S + E), where R=results, S=strategy, and E=execution. Without t, which equals 'trust', results = strategy plus execution. This is logical. You must have a good strategy and you must execute that strategy well in order to produce results. In this formula though, trust is a force multiplier. If trust is positive, then results are exponentially better. If trust is negative, then results are exponentially worse.

Think about the truth of this concept. If trust is high in your enterprise or positive, aren't changes and adjustments easier to execute? They get you on the adjusted path quicker than if trust did not exist or was impaired. On the other hand, if trust is not good, then changes or adjustments require all sorts of gyrations and meetings just to get the first edge of change accepted. Given similar strategies and abilities to execute, the enterprise with the greatest level of trust among its people has a faster pace and a far greater chance of success.

Trust is the most critical element of enhancing cooperation. 'Zoomers' require it and have a hyper-sensitivity to the lack of it. You would do very well to build trust at every opportunity and protect it with your life.

OTHER CONTEMPORARY THINKING

JAMES AUTRY

James Autry, former business executive, author, and now leadership consultant to some of the best corporations in America, captured my attention with his innovative leadership thinking in *Love and Profit*; two words you rarely, if ever, see together. The title got my attention. The sub-title is *The Art of Caring Leadership*. As one who speaks from big time executive experience, his insights into counter-cultural leadership were instrumental in the development of some of the concepts in this book.

His insights into trust; not being trustworthy, but trusting others, are simply true. He writes, "Everyone wants to believe that if people are trusted to do their work, they will do their work. And I do believe it, but believe me, trust is hard work and it's scary. Why? Because some people can't accept trust. Notice I did not say "can't be trusted" or "shouldn't be trusted." I said they can't accept trust. It is tempting to let this fact overshadow another fact: The great majority of people accept trust and thrive on it. So by the philosophy of managing for the good people, the most rewarding and productive attitude is to trust everyone. It is pragmatic as well, because not trusting people has no effect on those who can't accept trust but has a debilitating effect both on those who can – and also on you."

Oliver Wendell Holmes was quoted as saying, and I repeat this quote from my first book *ARISE!*, "I would not give a fig for the simplicity this side of complexity; but I would give my life for the simplicity on the other side of complexity." Leadership as the art of optimizing cooperation is essentially simple (not complex), but the work to get there is hard. What makes it hard is navigating through and fighting all the what-appears-to-be-normal thinking and biases that are based in the institutions around us. The battle to get to simplicity on the other side of complexity is worth the fight of your life.

"NEVER" POLICIES

Down turns in business, seasonal fluctuations, associated cost reductions, and unexpected customer churn are all part of any business' journey in the marketplace. Since there is no problem-free solution, it is important that the leader carefully select the set of problems he or she would prefer to solve. In my experience and opinion, the set of problems most likely to preserve cooperation is always the better set of problems to choose. This is also consistent with our definition of leadership as the *art of optimizing cooperation*.

I know you should never say, "never," but below are company policies and practices that can have a devastating effect on the cooperation of others, and ultimately on outcomes and results. Consequently, these policies and practices should rarely, if ever, be used without extraordinarily careful consideration and a clear understanding of how to mitigate their negative effect on cooperation.

Nepotism

I've worked in enterprises where family members of the owners were part of the business. I've also worked in enterprises where family members were not allowed to work in the business. There is a definite difference between the two. While family members might be wrongly disqualified from employment where a no nepotism policy exists, the set of problems created when an enterprise allows family members to work at the effort can be substantially greater.

After leaving the Air Force Academy, I enrolled at Baker University where my dad was professor and Chair of the Business School. This is as close as I have come to a nepotism-type issue involving me. My dad handled it well. He made no bones about it. If I were going to be in his class, which I was more than once, he made it abundantly clear that I would be handled more harshly and harder than other students to insure there was no perception of favoritism. He was intuitively conscious of the potential for problems and established a set of rules that insured I would receive, at best, fair treatment with the rest of the students.

Similarly, there is a significant counter-cooperative message sent to others when a family member is hired. The question everyone will ask is, "Why were they hired?" Was it because they were the best candidate? If they really were, then OK, but what are the chances that a family member is the best candidate out of all the hundreds of thousands of people qualified for the job? My intuition tells me that a family member is rarely the best candidate. If the family member is not the best candidate, then why were they hired? Is who you know more important than what you know? If the leader ever made results the critical target of effort, then this action speaks louder and quite contrary to achieving results. People now know the truth. If you hire a family member, the message you may be sending is, "The best candidate is not always hired or promoted and who you know is more important than what you know." Neither of these will help an enterprise optimize results, and both will kill cooperation and the commitment of others toward the work. If you can avoid nepotism, adopt a no nepotism policy and comply with it now.

Across-the-Board Compensation Decreases

Compensation is a tool for cooperation, so any changes related to compensation need to be taken very seriously. When enterprises struggle, many choose the institutionalized strategy of reducing salaries and wages across-the-board. What message do you think others receive with this practice? Sure, one message is that the situation is grave and that everyone should be willing to share in any adjustment. Unfortunately, the history of our business institutions tell us that not everyone participates (the executives), and if they do, not in an equitable fashion.

If your enterprise needs to reduce salaries and wages in order to compete, the executives must take the first decrease if cooperation is going to be optimized during this time. Additionally, doing an across-the-board decrease indicates that everyone has contributed equally to this situation. Is this really true? I contend that it is rarely true. If a business is failing, is it the line workers' fault or does responsibility lie somewhere north of there?

This situation offers a great time to trim the marginal performers. Why not eliminate or cut the wages and salaries of 'C' players and hold the wages of the 'A' and 'B' players? Wouldn't that keep your best players on the field? When I have been faced with this situation, I have always made it known, "Now is not the time to either be underutilized or the worst performer in your area of work. If you are, your employment is at serious risk." This keeps the priority on results, puts better performers at ease, and puts poorer performers on notice. All three of these will optimize commitment from those committed to the work.

Across-the-Board Compensation Freezes

Sometimes enterprises choose to freeze compensation across-the-board in addition to decreasing salaries and wages across-the-board. This, too, is a dangerous practice. This sends a message that, again, everyone contributed to the situation in equal measure. Is this really true?

If you do this to your best performers, guess who is likely to disengage from the work or leave? Your best performers! If results matter, then do the hard work of surgically freezing wages and salaries and rewarding those performing. Freezing compensation across-the-board is easy to implement by leadership, but has the worst effect on cooperation. Like so many decisions leaders can make, where the easiest road is taken, the hardest or worst effect on cooperation is usually recognized. Leadership is hard so leave the hard work with leadership. Do the hard work of reviewing everyone's performance and surgically and accurately assigning freezes. Start with the executives. This will optimize cooperation and results, even in times of trouble.

Across-the-Board Hiring Freezes

You are probably feeling that I think across-the-board anything is probably not a good idea. You are right! Leadership requires much more work than that if cooperation is to be optimized, regardless of the circumstance. I understand that where a business is shrinking or revenue growth has slowed that hiring people must be done carefully. Doing things carefully is not equivalent to doing things easily. Why would any enterprise focused on results not hire in areas where investment was needed to stop the slide or reverse the trend? Even employees know this, so when a mandate like this is handed out, people begin questioning the competence of the leaders.

A mandate from the top to freeze hiring takes a key results-related decision out of the hands of those who are supposed to be accountable for results. By taking away potential means, the accountability for results now moves to those issuing the mandate. This can have a lasting effect well beyond the situation requiring drastic measures. If later, results are substandard and consequences are levied, might the fault be inappropriately assigned to those who couldn't hire, causing a diminishing effect on cooperation with those who knew of the mandate? I think it would.

It is much better to send messages to those leading those engaged in the work like, "Be creative. Invent ways to do more with less. If you must hire, insure that there is a substantial immediate return on the investment. Only hire when all other options are exhausted." These messages emphasize both the gravity of the situation, and leave the accountability where it belongs. If you choose to do otherwise, against these "never" policies, be very, very conscious of the very real impact your actions have on the cooperation of others. Your actions will make a difference on results and outcomes.

THE PRACTICAL APPLICATION OF LEADERSHIP

We have spent time looking at a different kind of leadership from afar. We are now ready to take our first steps on this far shore. Leadership defined as the art of optimizing cooperation is not just a mental exercise. It is a foundational paradigm that allows leaders to think and behave in such a way to both optimize cooperation and to multiply leadership in others. It takes practice to master.

The remainder of this book is dedicated to illustrating the practical application of leadership as the art of optimizing cooperation. From these examples, executives and managers can learn how different the lenses of cooperation are when making decisions. It will take practice to get used to wearing these new lenses, but the discomfort will ultimately become a significant advantage for the executive who, and the enterprise that masters getting employees to fully and willingly commit to the work.

In the following pages are several real-world cases illustrating scenarios that happen to leaders and executives in the course of weeks, months, and years in an enterprise. The leader responses are tailored to the specific case scenario, but the thinking can be applied at any and all levels of an enterprise. Just change the names and positions. The paradigms illustrated will tend to optimize cooperation regardless of its use at a supervisory, managerial, or executive level. Leadership happens best with practice. The lens through which you view circumstances makes the difference in your response. Your response makes the difference in whether cooperation is optimized or diminished.

In each scenario, we pose the following:

Real-life Circumstance:

We pose a specific situation that leaders at multiple levels of an enterprise are likely to experience.

Likely Learned Response:

All of us have been taught to handle situations that arise in ways that best serve the beliefs and paradigms other than those of optimizing cooperation. You will likely find these responses common and familiar.

Preferred Response to Optimize Cooperation:

Here is where we break ties with old and tired beliefs and paradigms and practice viewing the enterprise and results through the lenses of optimizing cooperation. You will find these responses challenging, yet intuitively aligned with optimizing cooperation. Substantial explanations are provided as well as key language that can help any leader learn to use the lenses of cooperation better.

COOPERATIVE COMPETENCY©

CASE #1 • PREVENTION VS. PROSECUTION

Real-life Circumstance:

Jason, an employee working in the receiving department, is suspected of stealing inventory.

Likely Learned Response:

Employee theft is a grievous act. Hopefully, a culture exists in your enterprise that encourages others to report suspicious activities. Most internal controls protect against individual theft but rarely do they protect against collusion; two or more people working together to steal. Regardless of how you are notified of the potential theft, it is likely you learned to respond in a way that focuses on proving the theft and prosecuting the guilty party.

Once you become aware of alleged theft, you are likely to notify Human Resources and Security, keeping those who know as few as possible in order to plan and execute a plan to catch the alleged thief in the act. The fewer who know, the better, right? As the sting develops, cameras are installed, e-mails are screened, and phones are monitored to the extent the law allows. Security is put on alert and the plan is executed. No one knows about the potential theft until enough evidence is gathered to fire and prosecute Jason or any other employee involved in the theft.

When Jason is let go, the department manager is finally informed, as are the executives. You are applauded for your sting strategy, courage, and the outcome. The news finally reaches the other employees and they are surprised that Jason was stealing. The other employees certainly understand the consequence of Jason's actions, but they are left with a deep concern. If the company can monitor all activities, e-mails and phone calls in a stealth mode, how do they know that the enterprise is not secretly monitoring all of their activity, including break room activity and private investigators watching personal lives outside of work?

The theft stopped. You were recognized and rewarded. Good outcomes, but the employees are now paranoid and afraid of what the enterprise might be doing secretly to watch them. They don't trust the enterprise because Jason was caught by stealth methods and the intent of those involved was proof and prosecution. Is this the priority of the company?

Where has the cooperation meter moved with the way this was handled?

Preferred Response to Optimize Cooperation:

Prevention is a better cooperative motive than prosecution when someone is suspected of stealing. Suspicion of stealing offers an invitation, if prevention is the goal, to intervene immediately with questions in an attempt to stop what might be happening. Prosecution, on the other hand, because evidence is being gathered, defers the questions and inquiries until a later date. Prevention activities will stop what is happening immediately and allows a leader to deploy overt teams to shore up internal processes and controls in plain sight of those possibly stealing. Prosecution activities are most likely done covertly so that those stealing can be caught through the gathering of evidence.

In this case, if Jason was subjected to prevention inquiries and expectations were re-clarified, do you think he would stop if in fact he was stealing? I think so. Might he be offended by the questions? Possibly, but enter the conversations without judgment yet. Acknowledge his presumed innocence, but that his name was mentioned in and around these activities. Remember, your enterprise is not a court of law. If prevention is what you are after, it is unlikely you will have to go to court. You might say something like this, "Jason, your name was mentioned as someone who may be involved in stealing inventory from the company. As you know, this is a serious accusation, and if we find it is true, the consequences will be severe. At this point, we have no reason to suspect your involvement other than the mention of your name. Whether you are involved or not, we are immediately strengthening security, installing cameras, and checking purses and bags at the employee entrances. If it is happening, we simply want it to stop. If are involved, we expect you to cease immediately and make amends. If you aren't involved, then you have nothing to worry about." Handling the theft scenario this way brings the problem to light immediately and gives the enterprise the best chance of stopping the theft at the earliest stage possible, minimizing future losses and improving results.

The discussion with Jason should be closed with a discussion regarding the knowledge of others who may be involved. You might use these words as you finish your communications with Jason, "Jason, if you are aware of the theft that may be occurring or if you know of others who are involved, I expect you to disclose what you know. Those you name will be given the same discussion you just received. If we later prove their involvement, they will receive the same severe consequences. If you know they are involved and choose not to disclose them to me, and we find out otherwise later, your employment will cease here. Is that clear? Again, we simply want the theft to stop, now. We value you as an employee, but this activity will not be tolerated."

How does handling a theft problem this way affect other employees who are an audience to these inquiries? Certainly, employees close to the inquiries will be impacted. If others are involved in the theft, they will get immediate knowledge of the extent to which the company is strengthening controls and security around inventory. This will mitigate the potential for future theft. How does a mindset of prevention vs. prosecution effect those close to the inquiries, but not involved? Handling a theft problem like this shows that the company will 1) follow-up on names mentioned associated with an unacceptable activity, 2) not rush to judgment of the employees, but make clear their expectations and the consequences if such activities are proven, and 3) avoid the trust problems associated with covert activities aimed at "catching" employees stealing. Though theft is a grievous act, cooperation can be enhanced and results optimized by a leader seeking prevention vs. prosecution.

I have had to instruct many leaders on using this method of dealing with any asset defalcation. Most want to rush to judgment. It's interesting and enjoyable to many to play detective for a while. This case, though, illustrates the harm that can be done by using covert methods of investigating employee behaviors. I have seen significant damage to cooperation when executives at companies I worked for used to bring in people under the guise of "consultant" to actually replace people on the way out of the company. Once people caught on, and a "consultant" would show up, what do you think happened? Most of these were really consultants, but everyone began wasting valuable hours trying to figure out who was being replaced. The loss of trust was costly when the company used covert methods of doing things. When attempting to optimize cooperation, it is always best to be brutally honest about the circumstance and equally as honest about future expectations. You will find most people will appreciate the honesty and you secure the trust of the work force for years to come.

COOPERATIVE COMPETENCY©

CASE #2 • COMPENSATION FAIRNESS QUESTIONED

Real-life Circumstance:

Brandon is upset that Jake, a co-worker who has been on the job less time, makes more than he does. *This type of issue arises at all levels of an enterprise. The thinking and responses outlined here can be used to enhance cooperation at every level.*

Likely Learned Response:

As most of our employee handbooks mandate, sharing one's compensation with another co-worker is a grievous violation of company policy. [Go find the wording in your employee handbook.] It is likely the punishment for such a crime is discipline that could lead up to and include termination of one's employment.

As a manager, we have been coached to respond with a comment like, "That information is confidential. What Jake makes is between Jake and the company. By the way, how did you find out what Jake makes?" (Brandon now starts to squirm because the company policy stick is about to be pulled out and used as a weapon!)

Based upon your firm stance on policy and obvious disgust for Brandon knowing what Jake makes, Brandon begins to back-pedal and realizes he has just put himself in jeopardy. He makes up some lame excuse meant to avoid the policy-stick punishment and goes back to his job. You relish in your toughness and firm stance, knowing you have followed the human resources book to the letter.

While you gloat, what do you think Brandon is thinking or doing? I would imagine that Brandon is gladly sharing his "near-death experience" with his friends and co-workers. And what do you think Brandon thinks of you? Do you think he is sharing, "Wow! Dave executed his response to my question just like the book said. I hope I can be like him someday. What a great boss!" Not likely. No, I would say he is likely spitting poison about you and the company, trying to stir up a mutiny because he knows you "hid" behind company policy because you are doing something so unfair that you dare not speak of it to anyone. Jake is the beneficiary of your preference and Brandon, among all others, must beware!

Was cooperation enhanced by this response?

Preferred Response to Optimize Cooperation:

Do you really believe people will not and do not share their compensation simply because it is a violation of company policy?! They will and they do. Is it advisable for employees to seek out what others make? No. The reason people seek out what others make is to find someone who makes more that they do, but doesn't deserve to. If they find someone making less that deserves less, their ego is fueled and they feel validated in some way. But when they find one person who "can't be making more than me," look out! They will feel slighted and you will have a potential problem. Nothing good comes out of someone seeking to find out what others make. So counsel employees otherwise, but expect that they will share compensation information.

Since it happens, you need to be prepared. When Brandon found out Jake was making more than him, through whatever nifty means he used (do the means really matter as long as Brandon didn't violate Jake's privacy or have unauthorized access to company records?), is the real issue Jake's compensation or your perceived unfairness? I contend the latter is the prevailing issue.

An effective leader, listening and observing through the lenses of optimizing cooperation, will recognize this question as one about the leader's fairness, not about another's compensation. By responding as if the issue is about another's compensation, with company policy, you do two things that destroy cooperation: 1) you didn't "hear" what the employee is communicating, so now you are a boss who "doesn't listen," and 2) you affirm the concerned employee's belief that you are, in fact, unfair. You can bet there is a large audience to your response as well. The audience includes all the people that Brandon told as he prepared to go to the mountain and talk to "the man," or "woman" as the case may be, about this most unfair practice of paying people more who have less time on the job.

Anytime an employee has a concern, as a leader determined to optimize cooperation, you must listen. Rarely is the employee communication about the context of what he or she is bringing up (in this case, compensation). It is usually about trust or fairness; things that make or break cooperation. So listen! Acknowledge and receive what the employee is saying first. Say something like, "Thank you for sharing your thoughts and feelings about this. It is important that you are comfortable letting me know when you or someone feels mistreated or slighted. That is not what we want. I hold you in high regard for coming here to share this with me." So far, so good toward optimizing cooperation.

Now it is important to place some "value stakes" on the playing field. "Value stakes" form the foundation for decision making and policy for an enterprise. For instance, depending on your enterprise's values, you might share with Brandon like this, "There are some values we uphold here at the company that I want to make sure we both understand. I hope you have heard these before. (If not, this may indicate another problem.) We have a performance-based compensation structure. That means that time in a job or time with the company is not the primary factor by which compensation is determined. Jake may have less time on the job and less time with the company, and he may make more than you if his performance is better. Let's take a look." You may have a circumstance where Brandon simply does not believe in the value of a performance-based compensation structure. In that case, misaligned values are rarely reconcilable and it may be best, if this is the underlying problem, that Brandon seek employment elsewhere, because this issue will arise again and again.

In order to respond well to Brandon at this point, you must have some metrics, either quantitative or qualitative that you can refer to. If you don't, you are not well prepared and your effort to prove your fairness may backfire. Pull out the last few months of reports or both Brandon's and Jake's performance reviews. Some of you are cringing now at the thought of sharing information about someone else's performance with another employee. Your intentions at this point are critical. Are you doing it to deflate or defame the employee whose record you are about to share or are you sharing evidence that there is a rhyme and reason to the way compensation rewards are shared? The latter must be your intent.

Look at the records together and identify gaps where the performances of both employees differ. Do this objectively and talk about the details and metrics with the concerned employee. During this part of your response, you are either going to validate the accuracy of Jake's compensation or validate Brandon's claim that he should make as much or more than Jake. What do you do if you find out Brandon is right? Based upon objective criteria and the performance-based compensation structure, Brandon should be making as much or more than Jake. Complicating this picture is the company policy that says performance evaluations and corresponding pay increases are done on an annual hire date basis and Brandon's hire date is 6-months away. Remember, your ultimate goal is to optimize cooperation! Give Brandon the deserved compensation increase now! Will you have to fight some battles in Human Resources or with your boss? Probably. Is it worth it? Let's take a look.

So Brandon goes up the mountain to "the man or woman" and returns with a deserved, objectively determined, compensation increase. I can envision Moses coming down from Mt. Sinai after having seen the burning bush and everyone rushing to him to ask what happened. Brandon responds something like this, "Dave actually listened to me. He mentioned the performance-based compensation structure at the company and then compared my performance with Jake's. Jake does pretty good, too! But, afterwards, he realized that Jake and I perform basically the same job at the same performance level, so he gave me a raise!" Was cooperation enhanced? Absolutely! Some of you may be nervous that others may now think that, "All I have to do is go to Dave and I will get a compensation increase," right? Trust this listening and objective evaluation process. In some cases, where people believe they perform better, you may have to give raises, in others you may not. Will it take time? Sure. Is it your job? You bet it is!

What if during the objective review, both you and Brandon come to the same conclusion that Jake performs better than Brandon in key areas? Try responding to Brandon like this, "Brandon, it's obvious that Jake outperforms you in some key areas. I want to see you be infinitely successful here, so let's agree on a plan to get that compensation increase you will deserve once you hit these key performance metrics. How can I help you?" This invitation sets the stage for a dialogue between you and Brandon that should yield a training or development plan for Brandon and a specific timeframe for reevaluation. Now Brandon returns to "his people."

What does he share? He might share something like this, "Dave actually listened to me. He mentioned the performance-based compensation structure at the company and then compared my performance with Jake's. Jake does pretty good, too! I think I can match or beat Jake and when I do, Dave committed to me that I will get a compensation increase." Was cooperation enhanced? Yes. Are results likely to improve? Probably, with Brandon's increased effort and training. Was fairness validated and were values upheld? Yes.

I recommend one last step. Leave your office and go mingle with Brandon's people and find out what was said after the meeting. Do two things: 1) find out how Brandon represented the discussion you had with him, and 2) share the same value stakes and thought process you shared with Brandon. In this way, concerned employees learn they must be honest when they return to "their people" and you get to share paradigms and values that provide the foundation for a productive and cooperative work environment. If you find that Brandon did not speak the truth about your exchange with him, it is critical you confront Brandon and ask him about his intentions. If his intentions were to paint you in a bad or different light, see Real-life Circumstance, *Employee Misrepresents His or Her Boss*.

Additional Thoughts:

There are several thoughts about compensation that are fundamental to keeping cooperative issues surrounding compensation at a minimum. The first is to understand and believe that compensation is a tool for cooperation. It is nothing else. As a tool, it should be used surgically and flexibly to enhance the commitment of others to the work at hand. Some will need to be compensated more and others less, but there are some distinct boundaries and rules that must be in place first in order to be flexible and fair.

The first guideline is what I refer to as *internal equity.* This term speaks to the relationship of compensation to roles and responsibilities. Within an enterprise, some roles and responsibilities will pay more than others. Roles requiring leadership or a high-degree of technical competency will tend to pay more, while roles that do not require leadership or a significant technical competency will pay less. Flexibility and fairness can exist as long as *internal equity* is not violated; that is to say that someone with less responsibility makes more than someone with more responsibility. If you really want to throw your enterprise into a tail-spin, violate this *internal equity* guideline.

This guideline has other implications that are important. If a new employee is hired and, due to market reasons, his or her compensation "stretches" or violates internal equity, you may have to adjust others to his or her compensation standard to maintain internal equity. I would not make this a guarantee, though, but you should absolutely look at the effect of doing this on cooperation within your enterprise. I guarantee you that others will find out what this person makes. If the new hire's role and responsibilities are lower than those who make less, you will do huge damage to cooperation and trust. For those who perform and have similar, if not greater responsibility, doesn't it make sense that they should make at or the same compensation for similar work as long as they are good performers? The market has told you what others will pay for talent and you just did it! How many times do companies watch their talent leave because they used too rigid of structures for compensation. Choosing this set of problems can be disastrous!

For the employee who is not paid as much as the incoming hire and who is not as stellar a performer, it is a great opportunity to discuss a development plan for improvement much like that illustrated in this example. Don't just give everyone an internal equity adjustment. Do it surgically to optimize cooperation! Keep your paradigm consistent so that others know what to expect the next time internal equity becomes a cooperative issue.

The issue of hiring someone from outside the enterprise leads us to a second compensation guideline that helps us enhance cooperation. We call this *external equity. External equity* is one's compensation compared to those in similar roles and responsibilities in similar industries across the marketplace. If you do not pay your people commensurate with what the market will bear, you will likely lose them. This is a critical barometer and boundary for compensation flexibility and fairness. Paying significantly over this boundary will likely increase your costs to the point of impairing your ability to compete. Paying significantly less than this will increase the likelihood of key employee turnover, causing unrest and disruption to your culture and potential mission-fit misses of people.

By the way, these rules apply to executive compensation as well, with one major exception that we have already covered. A post-modern on-lookers' view of executive compensation is tainted by the absurd compensation packages well publicized in the media. If an executive uses these benchmarks as an *external equity* guideline, then I can almost assure you that cooperation will be diminished. A more appropriate guideline, ignoring *external equity*, is the point at which people disengage from the work because they believe your compensation if not fair given the difference in your role and responsibility to others within the enterprise. This is especially true during times of down-sizing or laying off workers.

I know this is holy ground for executives, but this is where the rubber of optimizing cooperation meets the road of an enterprise mattering more than any one person, including an executive. What's wrong with accumulating cash in an enterprise? I just heard today that Garmin®, head-quartered in Olathe, Kansas, near my home town is sitting on $1.8 billion in cash. The company is debt free. Does it have some choices? You bet! They can issue dividends to shareholders. They can give Christmas bonuses to employees. They can give irrationally to a local charity. All these choices are available at a time when the world financial crisis has taken its toll on most businesses.

I have shared many times in this book that the concept of leadership as the art of optimizing cooperation is easy, but the work to get there is hard. This kind of decision for an executive is the hard work. It flies directly in the face of the business institutional paradigms and beliefs. What will you choose with what you now know? Remember, the 'zoomers' are watching . . .

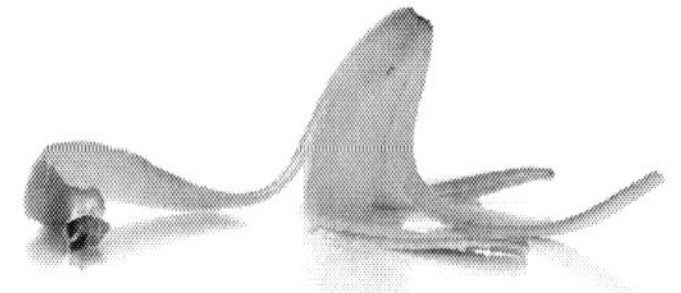

COOPERATIVE COMPETENCY©

CASE #3 • CONSISTENT APPLICATION OF COMPANY POLICY

Real-life Circumstance:

Angela, a single mom working for the company has been sick and absent from work beyond the number of policy days allowed. She is a good performer and respected team member. *This is but one example of how thinking around company policies is different when viewed through the lenses of cooperation. This thinking can be applied to any issues where company policy is violated or considered in making employee decisions.*

Likely Learned Response:

We are all taught as business professionals to apply policies consistently, right? The support for this consistency is the desire to mitigate the risk of law suits from employees who feel they have been mistreated or treated unfairly. The law protects employees from being treated unfairly due to race, gender, age, disability, or religious preference. By applying policies consistently, enterprises can minimize the risk of being exposed to unfair labor practices related to these prohibited criteria, but can a decision be made to enforce policy for another reason be acceptable?

Our Human Resources department will likely argue a decision like that cannot be made or can only be made if the legal risk is minimal. You will likely hear and think, "The policy is the policy." You will be coached to enforce it consistently across the board, regardless of the circumstance. In this case, you will prepare your documentation in advance and call Angela into your office. Since she is a good performer and respected by her peers, you will have mixed emotions, but the policy consistency rules dictate that you have this very difficult conversation with her. She probably expects something is coming since 1) she knows she has missed a lot of work due to the illnesses of her children, and 2) that others have been subjected to the consequence of separation when violating the attendance policy. You make your move, have the conversation, and escort Angela to the door. She waves sorrowfully to her team members, since she won't be given the chance to say her good-byes.

Now everyone knows that you, the boss, will enforce the attendance policy without favoritism or bias. You will not expose yourself to the risk of being unfairly discriminatory based upon the prohibited criteria of race, gender, age, disability or religious preference. As a matter of fact, you won't expose yourself to any risk; even that of being right and flexible with someone who deserves better!

You walk back to your office, on one hand feeling sad and sorry, but on the other hand feeling like you did your duty and the enterprise has been served better for the effort and boldness it took to let Angela go for a policy violation. A beer after work will take the guilty edge off and you'll be back at work tomorrow enforcing the same policies, insuring everyone is at work and on time. Management at its best!

It is likely Angela is disappointed, but understands. What about her coworkers? What do they think of you and the company? Do you think they know she was absent? You bet they do. They haven't seen her in several days. Do you think they know why she was absent? They probably know a lot more than you do, since the company's likely position is that the reason for an absence doesn't matter. Here's the truth and cooperative thread that is critical here. The reason for an absence doesn't matter to the company (you), but it matters immensely to Angela's co-workers. If they feel like and believe you have been unfair with Angela, they will cooperate less. Angela's co-workers know she was absent because the latest flu virus ran unabated through her and her three children over the last two weeks. Because her husband doesn't pay the required child support and because her hourly wage isn't a lot, she has not been able to afford day care for her sick kids, and even if she could afford it, it is unlikely the daycare would accept her sick kids. Angela was stuck like so many single moms.

In the infinite wisdom of applying a policy consistently, without regard to "why" the policy was violated, the leader damaged the cooperation of Angela's co-workers, having to have viewed the separation with little or no sensitivity for Angela's plight as a single mom. The irony of this incident is that the biggest damage to cooperation was done to those remaining at work. You've ignorantly created a beast within!

Preferred Response to Optimize Cooperation:

There is a rule of thumb regarding consistency that applies to any policy violation that will optimize cooperation and minimize legal risk. The rule of thumb is this: always apply the thinking process or spirit of a policy consistently, and let the outcomes vary according to circumstance. Let's examine Angela's situation through the lenses of cooperation, honoring and applying this rule of thumb.

If we begin with the end of this rule of thumb in mind, the circumstances surrounding a policy violation matter. Remember, the law prohibits unfairness based upon race, gender, age, disability, or religious preference, so these can never be considered in the circumstances of a policy violation. They are simply irrelevant to the decision. Notice that behavior, performance, trustworthiness, intentions or context are not prohibited from the decision. You can and should definitely use these in determining the consequences when a policy violation occurs if you desire to optimize cooperation.

In this case, Angela's context was the sickness of her children and her intentions being a single mom were to take care of them. I often think of single moms as the widows of today. They are as prevalent and as burdened as those spoken of in ancient communities. In many cases, their lives consist of one struggle after another. Angela's performance as an employee has been good. She is trustworthy and dependable beyond this recent illness of her children. She works well with her co-workers. Her behaviors at work and with and among her co-workers are acceptable. Her circumstance might be graded something like this:

Behaviors at work	B
Performance at work	A
Trustworthiness	A
Intentions	A
Context (of absence)	A

This combination of grades, or pattern of thinking, should generate a consistent consequence.

Someone with a similar sickness/absence circumstance but with performance grades like this might generate a different consequence:

Behaviors at work	C
Performance at work	B
Trustworthiness	B
Intentions	C
Context (of absence)	A

In this case, some form of discipline may be warranted.

You ask, "How do you know what to do when?" When faced with the same circumstance with two different people, the best barometer of what to do will be your answer to the question, "If I let this person go (remember, the policy provides for this option), will cooperation be improved or hindered?" If your answer is cooperation will be improved, let the person go. If cooperation will be hindered with your action, keep the person and communicate whatever you need to communicate to share the thinking pattern used and how it is applied fairly to all.

Ultimately, polices like these for attendance are useful because they give a leader an option for releasing a marginal or poor performing employee. Releasing an employee is only an option. A skilled leader knows when to use the policy "teeth" and when to pass on whatever prohibitions or disciplines the policy offers. Too many people hide behind these policies, much like the tenants of an institution that are the source of rebellion for so many 'zoomers,' using them indiscriminately to insure their consistent application. Using a policy like this to make the hard work of uniquely assessing each situation and employee easier, will send shock waves through the 'zoomers' within your employ and put your entire cooperative effort at risk. Leading is hard work. Quit trying to make it easy.

As an added and necessary benefit, the consistent application of the thought process will protect you from negative consequences of litigation. Perhaps counter-intuitively, you get more protection from this application of the consistency principle than you do from applying consistent consequences for policy violations because employees subject to the latter get incensed and often seek to get even for perceived wrong-doings by the company. The former offers a balanced, yet consistent approach that most employees will respect and support. Wouldn't you prefer the former application of the consistency principle; consistency in thinking versus consistency in consequences? I know I would.

COOPERATIVE COMPETENCY©

CASE #4 • CONFRONTING LACK OF COMPLIANCE

Real-life Circumstance:

Ron, a single male employee and mediocre worker, has not violated the company's attendance policies, but was seen outside of work and bragged about missing a required work day for the rest of his team.

Likely Learned Response:

Contrary to the previous scenario illustrated with a single mom who violated the attendance policy, our normal or learned response here is likely to be one of frustration with Ron, accompanied by little action because no policy was violated. Managers learn that they, for legal prudence reasons, are discouraged from acting on someone's poor decision making or poor judgment until a policy is violated. Others may choose to wait to confront Ron about his absence or decision just wanting to simply avoid the confrontation since policy can't be used to fire Ron. Does this sound like you?

Avoiding confrontations is indicative and an epidemic of poor leadership, if leadership is the art of optimizing cooperation. There are very few things that can hurt cooperation more than avoiding confronting others about their behaviors that damage cooperation. In a case like this, leaders will often give Ron the evil eye for a couple of days while he smirks with his peers about avoiding a mandatory work day, in the hopes that his behavior will change with the silent or "I'm angry so don't come near me," routine. A week or so from now, as politically astute as Ron is, he will come to you as a buddy and offer, "Hey, no hard feelings. I just had a commitment that I had to tend to. You know what I mean," in an attempt to further sand down your edges regarding what he did. You feel good that your relationship with Ron has mended and you are hopeful that the next mandatory day he will honor your friendship.

The next time, what does Ron do? His ploy worked the last time, didn't it? He was able to miss a mandatory work day and ease his way back into to your good graces. I bet he tries to miss again. Your evil eye gets harder, longer, but, eventually, Ron comes back all smiles and endears himself to you again; all to the disgust of those watching.

Who are those watching? Those watching are every employee who sacrificed their time and personal agenda for the mandatory work day. Most may not have known Ron had missed the day until someone spread the news that Ron was spotted driving golf balls at the local driving range right in the middle of the work day. They aren't angry, yet. They are anxious to see what you, the leader, will do. The workers perceive that you like Ron, because he has a way of skirting accountability a lot. They see your best Clint Eastwood evil eye, but see no significant consequence for Ron. On the contrary, they see you and Ron back in the same old groove as if nothing happened. Cooperation diminished. Attendance at the next mandatory work day is lower than normal as others test the accountability line. You now have a big problem with compliance to authority and results will suffer.

Preferred Response to Optimize Cooperation:

Why are you waiting to confront Ron with his poor decision? Must a policy violation exist before you intervene and act? Remember our discussion of a cooperatively competent leader's ability to 1) recognize a cooperative problem, 2) choose to intervene, and 3) handle the issue productively with the employee. This is a great example where the leader either failed to recognize the problem for what it really was, or chose not to intervene. Both are all too common.

Ron willfully violated your direction and expectations as the leader. He might as well have sawed your legs off at the knees because you are now two feet shorter in the eyes of the people you lead. He told you by his actions; public actions by the way; that he did not want to comply with your direction. Remember the first question in the accountability tool we studied? By not responding appropriately, with enough discipline to change the behavior, you have set the stage for the audience of other workers to engage less willingly and less fully in the work.

Here is the kind of response that will optimize cooperation of the audience of workers. Invite Ron with little fanfare into your office to discuss something. First, acknowledge his absence during the mandatory work day and seek to validate the news that he was seen at the local driving range during the mandatory work day. The last thing you want to do is falsely accuse someone of something they did not do. He will either confirm or deny it.

If he denies the accusation, it is time to set some very stern and deep value stakes. Saying something like this will speak clearly to Ron about this and future activity of this nature. "Ron, the next time we have a mandatory work day, I expect you here, on time and ready to work the entire day. Your team members expect that of you and it's fair. I do, too. If we ever see or confirm a team member is out in town, without a very, very good reason for missing a mandatory work day, the consequences will be severe enough to change the behavior, which could include elimination of one's employment. Is that clear?"

Finish the conversation by asking Ron if you need to document this in his employment file. If Ron says, "No," then confirm your trust in him verbally. It is highly unlikely that he will say, "Yes." If he does, explore why. You may end up terminating his employment immediately due to his unwillingness to commit to being there on the next mandatory work day. What about progressive discipline you ask? You already gave him an oral warning. He has told you he would like written documentation of this. The only level left is a suspension or termination. Progressive discipline does not have to take three months. It's still progressive discipline; even if it happens within the same five minutes!

If Ron confirms the sighting outside the office, begin by asking Ron questions about his level of commitment and indicate that his 1) lack of attendance, and 2) lack of respect for the request for a mandatory work day are serious problems. Explain to him that the audience to his behavior is very large, including his team members, and consequently, the discipline to correct the behavior is very important. Ask Ron what level of discipline he thinks needs to be issued to change the behavior. Isn't that all we need? You would be surprised that when the employee is holding the sword that kills themselves how honest they are about discipline and how committed they are to a different outcome thereafter.

Don't fire him immediately like some leaders do because they are so insecure about the power one employee exercised over them. Remember, 'zoomers' know they have power over you. *The fact is 'employees' have had power over employers for a long time. They are just now reaching critical mass in this information economy.* There is much more power is keeping the proverbial sword in its sheath versus pulling it out and using it.

To close your conversation with Ron, tell him that you expect him to share the level of discipline issued and the exchange of information with his teammates. They deserve that level of transparency and they need to rebuild their trust in Ron. If he defers to you, then you do so appropriately, emphasizing that you trust that this type of behavior will not be repeated. Also request that his teammates also trust and care for Ron. This is a strong and powerful way of insuring on-going cooperation, even in light of a bad circumstance.

Should you handle Ron any differently if he were a superior worker, based on the fear that Ron might leave if confronted with such an accusation? No, but many leaders do. They turn a blind eye to activities of those who perform well at work, yet make poor decisions otherwise. This creates perceptions of favoritism and bias that can ruin cooperation very quickly. I once had a manager who simply would not confront one of our most productive workers. She was very efficient, yet she was constantly stirring up mistruths in the workplace. He would just turn a blind eye to her. After seeing and hearing enough, I told him between the thin whiteness of my lips, "I want the head of the snake removed, now. Who is it?" He told me it was this lady, which I already knew. With my pressure, he finally did what he needed to do.

There are multiple problems here that all worked themselves out. The fact that he would not intervene without pressure from me indicated a leadership problem that ultimately cost that manager his job. It wasn't this instance that caused him to lose his job. It was the continual choice to not intervene in cooperative issues. The lady's employment was separated, much to the surprise of the rest of the workers. They, too, knew she was very productive, but that she also was a fascist in the workplace. This sent a very loud signal to them about how important cooperation is to the effort. Any thoughts of continuing the destructive behavior she exhibited was squelched then and there.

And the lady who was let go … years later she was rehired as a more mature person and she is currently a supervisor at the same company. Now that's a win, win, and win! Optimizing cooperation is hard work, but it pays off in spades.

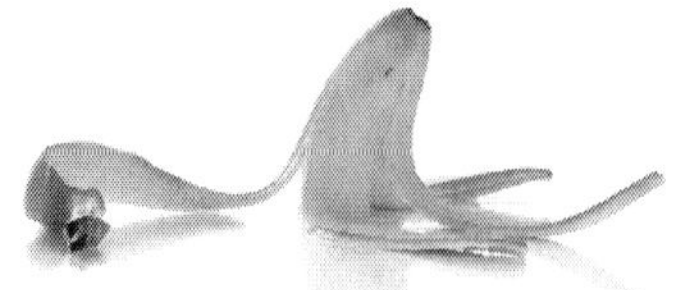

COOPERATIVE COMPETENCY©

CASE #5 • PAYROLL ADJUSTMENTS IN DECLINING BUSINESS

Real-life Circumstance:

Revenues are down and all departments are asked to cut 10% off their annual payroll budget. Robert, a 'zoomer,' is one of the least senior members of the team, yet performs near the top by objective measures.

Likely Learned Response:

A declining business environment is difficult, no matter where or when it occurs. This is a common time when enterprise leaders develop reputations for coldness, heartlessness, or sometimes the more honorable "steely resolve." In this kind of scenario, managers often strap up their boots high and tight and do the dirty work expected of them. It is not pleasant, but a seasoned, trained manager will take the mandate and do it; most of them totally ignorant of the mandate's effect on cooperation.

If you are like most managers, in knowing and anticipating having to deliver bad news, you intentionally show some physical signs of what is to come; revealing the prophecy in your furrowed brow, defeated posture, and your quietness relative to your normal demeanor. Usually, this kind of mandate comes at a time after the business has struggled awhile and people are aware and concerned about the consequences of diminishing company financial performance. Your demonstration confirms their greatest fear, "Something's goin' down, and it ain't good." In a prophetic way, your demeanor eases the burden of direct and prompt communication.

Robert, aware of his excellent performance because he gets rave reviews and receives frequent accolades, is expecting to avoid any type of negative effect to his personal compensation or position because the company promotes its pay-for-performance system widely. As you sit down to plan your budget reduction strategy, you look at names and positions as thoughts like these enter your head; "Ron's been here a long time. There is no way he could be cut;" "Joan is the only person who knows what's going on in that department. She can't be cut;" "Omar has a complaint filed with HR about harassment. We can't cut him." "Robert is the newest employee on our team. He was looking for a job months ago. He can look for another one. He might be someone we could cut." All the exceptions and reasons for cutting out individuals lead you to the decision to give an across the board pay decrease of 10%. You wrestle with cutting your own pay because you make just enough to cover your bills on a monthly basis as it is. The mandate didn't include you, so you do precisely what was asked of you; cut 10% off your payroll expenses. Your compensation is part of someone else's budget line item. You think, "Hopefully they'll let go another manager like Tom, who has been here less time than me."

Having made this decision, you sulk for a day or two so that those around you can prepare for the news to come which can't be good, because you are so down. You think, "The longer I sulk, the more people will dread. The more people dread, the better they will handle some bad news because people always expect the worst when bad news is forthcoming."

When the day comes to announce the 10% pay cut for everyone, you let everyone know that the "budget" forced the pay across-the-board pay adjustment. Just prior to the meeting with your employees, you were relieved to learn that one of your peer managers was let go and your pay was left untouched. The employees react with cool resignation during the meeting, having thought that many would be let go all together. Your plan to settle them with time and sulking worked like a charm. They were accepting of the change, though expectedly disappointed. After the meeting, you send everyone back to work and return to your office with a feeling of accomplishment, having done your duty and having survived another rough management task. At least for the moment, your ignorance of this decision's effect on cooperation appears to have been inconsequential, until next week . . .

Preferred Response to Optimize Cooperation:

On the surface, the scenario above appears to be executed reasonably well, with little diminishing effect on the cooperation of the workers. Let's look a little closer to the management behaviors exhibited and their effect on cooperation. First of all, these types of tough financial performance times are part of the lifecycle of any enterprise. Sometimes they are predictable with a season and others they come between success and the innovation of the next big thing. Being prepared to, not just survive these times, but enhance cooperation in these times is a significant competitive advantage.

Enhancing cooperation begins long before this day comes. Employees should be made aware of company financial performance and how each of the jobs makes a difference in that financial performance. Employees should also know the basis on which compensation is determined; longevity, tenure, utility, performance or something else. It's good that the poor company financial performance is not a surprise. The first step in a poor financial performance scenario likely to result in payroll adjustments is to communicate honestly the rationale to be used to make such adjustments. Because the financial performance is not a surprise, being forthright with the employees about what will happen when, helps build credibility and trust. Sulking and pouting just create anxiety in all those watching. The behaviors are too vague and abstract, though negative.

Because I believe in performance based compensation systems, I have always shared comments like, "For those of you poor or mediocre performers, this is not the time to be the lowest performer on the list. When we make decisions about who to keep, we keep the best performers. You had weeks and months to improve. Your efforts to improve will be a significant element in making these tough choices. Unless we can't make selective reductions due to job specialization or loss of critical mass, an across-the-board pay reduction technique will not be employed. Those of you on the upper end of the performance scale can keep doing what you're doing." These words keep your best performers less anxious and focused on performance while your mediocre and poor performers have reason to worry.

Your next step is to minimize the time between explanation and adjustments. Anxiousness has a way of quickly creeping into the culture and poisoning even those who have few worries. I recommend getting rid of your poor performers and mediocre-to-low employees first and quickly. This validates your intentions explained above and builds trust. If you must still cut others, I recommend focusing on your good, but under-utilized employees. It is important that you explain why these folks were chosen to be let go. In most cases, a few full-time roles that can be absorbed by others, helps retain the core of your good-to-excellent work team.

When you talk to the individuals being let go, don't explain that the "budget" was the reason for letting someone go. "Budgets" are never a reason to do something. They are only an accelerator. The reason people were let go in this scenario is because their relative performance to others was low. The separation was accelerated by the budget problems. This leaves the control of performance where it belongs; with the employee. It was them, not you, who set the stage for separation.

There is one BIG thing a leader can do that makes a scenario like this easier and helps minimize the damage to cooperation. Just because your compensation may be on someone else's budget line item, optimizing cooperation would dictate that you share in the payroll reductions FIRST. Most company's poor financial performance cannot be laid at the feet of people pushing the rocks. More often than not, the accountability for company financial performance rests at the top. Compensation adjustments should match accountability levels. This makes conversations with others easier and protects trust and cooperation when (notice I didn't say, 'if') employees find out who shared and did not share in the adjustments. You do not want to be on the list of those who did not share, even if you voluntarily have to cut your pay.

How do you think Robert, who performs near the top of the performance scale yet is new to the team, would respond to the 10% across-the-board pay cut? If he had heard about and believed in the company's performance-based compensation system, I would imagine he would be shocked, disappointed, and angry. Because Robert is a zoomer, he tweets and text messages anyone within an earshot about how unfair the company has been; not because of the poor financial performance, but because the company did not honor its word of prioritizing performers. Credibility and trust would have been lost, and, likely, lost for good. Odds are, performers perform worse because there is no perceived benefit for performing otherwise.

"Budgets" are never a reason to do something. They are only an accelerator. The reason people were let go in this scenario is because their relative performance to others was low.

Handling this scenario as suggested to optimize cooperation, Robert would have likely felt more secure and, when he observed poorer performers being let go first, he would at least feel some comfort that the company does what it says it will do; honor performance. Making performance the reasons for letting others go sets performance as a high value stake. Your participation in the adjustments indicates your belief that you own your part of the financial performance. Trust and cooperation are enhanced, even through a difficult time.

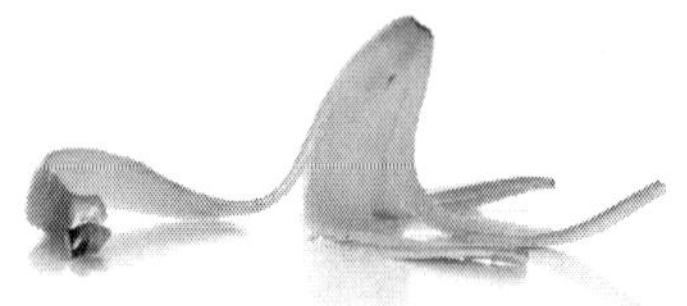

COOPERATIVE COMPETENCY©

CASE #6 • FRIENDS DON'T LET FRIENDS GO

Real-life Circumstance:

Josh is a long-time friend and confidant of the company President. Josh's performance is mediocre, at best, and the team doesn't care much for him. Tightening budgets have required cuts in personnel.

Likely Learned Response:

This is a thorny scenario. Josh is a personal friend of yours. People know it and you make no attempt to hide it. You are frequently seen in one another's offices after hours reminiscing about old times and the scuttle-butt in the neighborhood. Josh is employed because of his specific competency, but it's obvious that you and Josh have a relationship based on something other than just work.

The decision to cut personnel is always difficult and is made doubly difficult when you know and care for someone in the enterprise. You risk a lot if you let Josh go; not just a collegial relationship, but a long-time friendship. You do everything possible to avoid Josh's name appearing on a "hit list." Your mind can't fathom what that conversation might be like. For all practical purposes, you have been Josh's sponsor and he has been your confidant; the one person with whom you share your highest highs and lowest lows.

As meetings about tightening the budget continue, you are pleased that Josh's name does not appear on any "potential" list. You are relieved he has "made it." Weeks later, after all the decisions have been made, people are notified of their outcome and those selected are asked to leave. Those leaving feel disappointed, but they understand. Those staying feel a sense of relief and continue working as they have done before. Everything is fine, or so it seems . . . You didn't have to have that most undesirable conversation with Josh, and those remaining are continuing to work, but the undertow of damage to cooperation is about to be revealed.

Preferred Response to Optimize Cooperation:

Close relationships based on something other than the work in an enterprise can blind a leader from the effect on cooperation of a decision or the lack thereof. In this case, a concern for the cooperation of others in the work never entered your consciousness. Consequently, your decision to either protect Josh, or, certainly not to offer Josh as a potential casualty of tightening budgets, could have had devastating effects on cooperation. Josh's mediocre performance did not enter your mind. What others thought if Josh was retained with his mediocre performance never entered your mind. The level of engagement of others in the work if Josh was let go due to his mediocre performance in times like these didn't enter your mind. You were solely concerned with the conversation you did not want to have with Josh, and it hurt you and the enterprise significantly.

What do you think those let go think of Josh? Protected? Special? Your favorite? Probably. Do you think those remaining employed think any differently? Probably not, and they think much more. By not considering Josh a potential person to be let go, you acknowledge and affirm many value stakes in the culture of the enterprise. Here are just a few:

- Who you know is more important that what you can do.
- Mediocre work performance is acceptable here.
- Popularity (knowing the boss) is key to protecting your status.

None of these will breed optimal results. Quite the contrary. You have set the stage for years of beliefs consistent with these value stakes. Was the conversation you so desperately wanted to avoid with Josh worth the work environment you just created?

And remember, the zoomers are already texting and tweeting about the fact that Josh is still at the company and how his relationship with you was more important than performance. A leader practicing leadership as the art of optimizing cooperation would have considered both Josh's performance in these decisions, as well as the likely reaction of the audience (other workers) to either Josh leaving or Josh staying. In the companies I have led, I have referred to the selection of someone to leave as, "ringing the bell." In many enterprises and obvious to most, the boss can "ring the bell." What is less obvious and very critical in a culture and workplace where cooperation reigns and results matter is that the audience (other workers) can "ring the bell" on someone else. Often times I have told those being let go that their peers "rang the bell" for them; that their peers no longer wanted to work with them due to their performance. It's a sobering message to receive, especially from your peers.

The idea of letting others "ring the bell" on a peer may bother you. Let's look deeper at the thinking behind this idea. First of all, in order to give this opportunity to the audience, you must trust the audience to make objective, work-related, and performance-related decisions. If the culture is healthy, the audience will know the basis for decisions. If you balk at giving the audience this authority, then perhaps what is invisible, unwritten, and unspoken that governs behavior is more powerful than it ought to be. Clarify the culture.

Second, by allowing the group to participate in these decisions, they get to understand and feel the weight of these decisions. It is also likely that you will get to coach them as they may roll in some less-than-objective assessments of the team member in question. This coaching can re-affirm beliefs and paradigms within the enterprise and help you develop other leaders.
Third, this level of involvement builds trust. Employees can empathize with others being considered for separation. They usually take these situations very seriously and often direct resources at investing in peers before "ringing their bell." Isn't this the way it's supposed to work! There are no excuses in a work place like this. Your performance is your performance.

In an environment and culture like this, it is likely someone would have brought Josh's name up in one of the meetings, referencing his mediocre performance. If you defend him without objective and observable cause, you will have damaged cooperation. If you ask objective questions of the one nominating Josh with the intent of assessing his or her thinking pattern and find it to be sound, leaving Josh on the list enhances cooperation. Your personal anxiety over an impending conversation with Josh has no bearing. The concept of leadership as the art of optimizing cooperation is not complex, but the work to get there is hard.

COOPERATIVE COMPETENCY©

CASE #7 • EMPLOYEE MISREPRESENTING HIS OR HER BOSS

Real-life Circumstance:

Jessica has chosen to misrepresent a conversation she had with you because the outcome was not what she wanted. *Like in Case #2, this circumstance can arise after any meeting with you, the leader. If you don't follow-up to observe how your conversation was represented to others, cooperation can be damaged significantly. Yes, it takes time, but convincing others of the truth later will take a lot more time.*

Likely Learned Response:

The most likely and prevalent learned response will be to trust the employee to represent you fairly. We have spent lots of time emphasizing how important it is to trust others, right?! So most of us would have a conversation and let the employee represent what was discussed and the related outcomes as he or she sees fit.

If the conversation between you and Jessica is, in fact, represented fairly, then you have no worries. But if Jessica misrepresents what was you said or discussed, you may have a serious problem. The first questions if you do not follow-up is, "Will you know how the conversation was represented to others by Jessica? If so, then how will you find out? From another employee?" Maybe, but only if the culture is open and honest. If you go hunting for evidence of a misrepresentation long after the fact or without telling Jessica that you will follow-up, it looks like you are leading a witch hunt. This will shut everyone up.

But what about trust, you ask? Trust well-placed is critical, but where the potential to damage cooperation is very high, follow-up is just as critical. By not following up, you leave your fate in the hands of someone who may not be accepting of the outcomes you discussed.

When you hear of the misrepresentation, you might be tempted to dismiss the person unceremoniously because the conversation may have been misrepresented more than slightly. Some of you will "consider the source" and, knowing the truth, remain silent about it. Others will directly confront Jessica publically to ask her, "What did you say to your co-workers?" causing public embarrassment and pressure. All of these will damage cooperation.

Preferred Response to Optimize Cooperation:

By not following-up or following-up inappropriately, you set the stage for serious damage to cooperation and miss a huge opportunity to affirm communication channels and uphold the spirit of cooperation real-time. The best thing to do when you hear of the misrepresented conversation between you and Jessica as you follow-up the conversation is to ask Jessica to meet with you in a private area where you can discuss her activity discretely.

Do not jump to conclusions! You only heard she misrepresented the conversation. You don't know if she actually did, yet. Tell her that during your follow-up, to which you eluded at the end of your conversation with her, you heard a story being told that did not represent the truth as you recall it. Ask her to repeat what she told others and reaffirm that it is more-than-OK to tell others, but the truth must be told, not some twisted version of the facts. Listen and measure what you hear against what you originally said and against what the employee you asked heard from Jessica.

If Jessica is forthright about her misrepresentation, ask her about her motives for doing so. She may have been upset at the outcomes and felt as if twisting the conversation with her peers evened some kind of score with you. Remember, you still have the sword at your side. Leave it sheathed for now. She may have forgotten the facts. (I know you must think I am naïve with that last comment, but it's better to get the message across that misrepresentations will not be tolerated than to corner the employee is such a way that the fate of admitting a wrong doing outweighs any correction.) I call this kind of response a "fate worse than death" response, and I have seen many a manager or employee make a decision to go down the ship rather than admit a mistake.

In Sun Tzu's *The Art of War*, one significant lesson is, "Never surround your enemy." If you surround your enemy, they will likely fight to the death. Unless you are willing to die or kill someone, figuratively of course, give your enemy, or in this case, your employee, a way out that preserves his or her dignity. Let the possibility that Jessica might have forgotten the facts stand and ask her to go back to anyone and everyone she talked to and correct the facts. Believe me, this is a much worse fate than having to admit she intentionally misrepresented you!

Follow-up with others again and insure she knows you will. Thank her for being honest, even if you doubt that she forgot. She will appreciate the grace shown her and is not likely to "forget" again. Of course, if this is the third or fourth time Jessica has forgotten facts after having a conversation with you, you may need to pull the sword out and end the relationship based upon a lack of trust. If trust has been placed as a significant value in the enterprise, continued doubt about one's intentions should be dealt with quickly and deliberately.

There is a subtle, but significant difference in handling this separation, if Jessica has a history of misrepresenting you and the facts. What would be the reason you document for her separation? Most would say lying or misrepresenting the facts. I would record it as a *lack of trust* based upon frequently misrepresenting the facts. She is being let go because she can't be trusted, not because she misrepresented someone. Think about those close to Jessica who might think she was separated for speaking truthfully about you in a negative way. What if she was right?! What if you did mishandle a situation? It happens. Don't you want people to give you feedback in that scenario? If you separate people for misrepresenting the facts, you will likely cut off a critical communication channel when you mishandle something. Make the separation about not trusting, not misrepresenting.

Of course, if Jessica is not forthcoming with her misrepresentation, disclose the value stakes clearly and definitively, as if she had done it. It's good for her to hear of the consequences for such actions and to hear the expectations going forward. If the misrepresentation is grievous, then it may be appropriate to get Jessica and the person who heard what Jessica said in the same room in order to get to the truth. This can be very tricky, as one or both may feel surrounded because someone is about to get caught in a lie. It is unlikely a peer would intentionally misrepresent what Jessica said about your meeting. The ability to let employees know you are dead serious about cooperation is critical to its manifestation in the work place.

After this kind of an exchange, it is likely appropriate to follow-up with each individual to let them know how important trust is and that trust still exists, but that future occurrences like this will diminish trust and may result in separation of employment based upon an inability to trust.

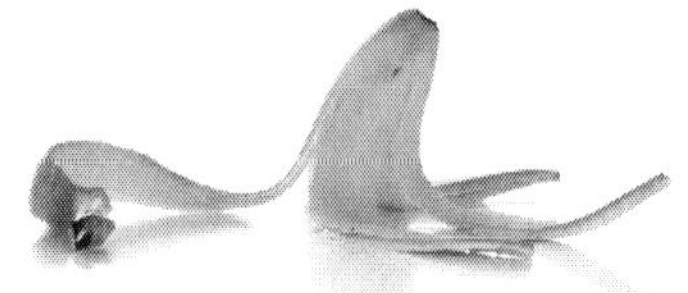

COOPERATIVE COMPETENCY©

CASE #8 • INCAPABLE, UNDER-PERFORMING MANAGER

Real-life Circumstance:

Brent is a relatively new manager and has under-performed for months under your leadership. Others are putting pressure on you to do something about him.

Likely Learned Response:

This scenario is not uncommon at all. Things like this often happen when the Peter Principle manifests itself in the workplace. The Peter Principle holds that "you are promoted to your level of incompetence." That means that where you stop is one notch above where your maximum capabilities are.

It is common for leaders to promote their best "doer" to a position of supervision or management. And it is common for the best "doer" to want that kind of promotion. The mutual desire often makes a promotion decision easy. Without proper training and leadership or management skills development, it is likely the promoted will perform just like Brent; not so good.

Perhaps you've tolerated Brent's under-performance and chalked it up as his "learning curve" while those subject to Brent's leadership have suffered.

Finally, after hearing the cries of his people, you begin a path of progressive discipline that you hope will turn Brent around. You have a conversation with Brent as an oral warning. Brent promises to do better and he exhibits to you that he wants this job. After a few weeks, his performance is no better, so you call him in again and give him a written warning. He looks defeated. He tells his friends how rough you are on him and tells them, "Can't (you) see how hard he is working?!" A few weeks pass. No improvement is noted, so you fire Brent.

You figure you've responded well to the pressure put on you by others to do something with Brent. While it was tough, you did the job a good manager should do. You responded to a point of pain and got rid of it. In the meantime, those who watched as you figuratively kicked and prodded Brent to perform while he was working so hard, do not think so highly of you. "He was trying so hard! I guess hard work is not appreciated around here."

Preferred Response to Optimize Cooperation:

The very first thing a leader must do when confronted with a negative observation is go to the Accountability Diagram in the Cooperative Competency© chapter. The first question to ask is, "Does the employee want to?" In the likely learned response, you either neglected Brent's exhibit to you that he "wants to" or you didn't consider his promise to do better worthy of consideration. It is not uncommon to get this kind of response from someone who is trying very hard to be successful. They are being honest! They really, really want do better and are working very hard at it. This kind of a response should indicate a very strong 'yes' to question number one.

Given this answer, discipline is not the proper tool. What do you think Brent thinks of your oral warning when he is working so hard to perform? I imagine he is not happy, and I imagine he has told those close to him that he is not happy. You do not discipline someone who wants to do the work. Cooperation is diminished when you do.

The second question is, "Can the employee do the work?" His lack of performance coupled with his obvious desire to do the work points to him not being capable of doing the work. You will have to assess if Brent has the requisite skill set for the role to which he has been assigned. If you think he does, then move to the third question, "Can the process be enhanced?" This often includes training and skills development. In this case, he may have been promoted too fast without the requisite skills training. You can go back and try to develop the needed skills in him. If his poor performance continues, you will go back around the diagram to the second question again. Can he do the work? At some you point you will arrive at a, "No."

Consistent with the diagram that helps us to optimize cooperation when a negative observation is made, your job now as his leader is to find a place for Brent to be successful. This is not a disciplinary move. This is a move to retain someone who is fully and willingly committed to the work and help them be successful. While Brent may be disappointed with a move like this, because he really wanted to be successful, this move will likely relieve his anxiety and give him the confidence to be successful. He retains his employment, you have been fair, and his co-workers appreciate having Brent around. Cooperation is enhanced.

Confirming that someone promoted cannot do the work, even with great effort, is a difficult and emotional discussion. The person receiving the news that they cannot do the work will be disappointed and likely tearful. Be prepared to care for them and acknowledge their strengths and the value of their commitment. The most tearful discussions I have ever had surrounded these types of discussions. But I've also seen where people have finished their careers feeling validated and valued, after having been removed from a position to which they were once promoted.

Handling someone who is not capable of performing the role assigned like this will optimize cooperation. Too many leaders refuse to make this adjustment because their intuition tells them that discipline is not the answer. Their intuition is right! But you still must make the adjustment to optimize results. Do it under the guise of retaining a committed employee and finding him or her a place where he or she will be successful. Your entire enterprise will be better for it.

CLOSING THOUGHTS

And so we have explored the far shore . . .

We've defined the problem catalyzing this 'zoomer rebellion' as one based in fighting institutions meant to mirror truth, but pale in comparison to the truth.

We've acknowledged that 'zoomers' want the truth beyond and behind the institution and they will fight for it!

We've defined leadership as **the art of optimizing cooperation**, honoring the principle that, "Two are better than one because they have a good return for their work."

We've provided five things that leaders **do** to optimize cooperation:

- Think strategically
- Create purpose
- Secure essential resources
- Define communication channels
- Identify and develop other leaders

We've provided a problem solving and accountability methodology that, when followed, optimizes cooperation.

We've developed an understanding of how important trust is in gaining the full and willing commitment of those considering joining the work.

We've shared some "never" policies that will almost always damage cooperation.

We've high-lighted some other contemporary opinions on leadership and woven their truth into the beliefs and paradigms in this book.

And, finally, we have provided practical cases where the lenses and language of optimizing cooperation are illustrated.

The next move is yours. Much like the early explorers, those first landing on the far shore had to decide whether to stay and make a life in the new world, or return to the near shore, perhaps to bring others along on this adventure, or perhaps to return to what is comfortable and more understood. Those who return will leave treasures unknown. Those who stay and practice leadership of a different kind will leverage the work force of today and tomorrow; the 'zoomers;' and reap yet unforeseen competitive advantage in the marketplace of the 21st Century.

The **slide** of American enterprise leadership will not be stopped or reversed if everyone returns to the near shore. Some must stay and practice and teach and test and explore further this new landscape. Maps of this new land must be drawn for those sure to come. Boats and bridges must be built. I encourage each of you to stay here and practice what will be normal tomorrow; leadership as the art of optimizing cooperation.

IF YOU ARE INTERESTED . . .

The strength and character required to lead in the 21st Century is substantial. Whenever a leader goes up against the inertia of decades and centuries of thinking, the battles are sure to be cataclysmic. This is world-changing work!

Some of you reading this book may have already connected the dots between the beliefs, paradigms, and behaviors described in this book and the Christian faith. These practices are for any and all leaders because they work. For those of you who follow Christ, leadership practiced as the art of optimizing cooperation is fully aligned with our faith and Biblical truth.

If you are interested, my first book, *ARISE! Life-changing Truths for the Tormented Leader* helps connect the dots between God and work. With the 'zoomer' rebellion against institutions, not the least of which is the church, alignment of beliefs and values across life contexts is critical to earning the trust of 'zoomers' and the world. Too many Christ-followers never connect the dots between God and work, leaving doubt in many about the existence of God and the relevance of God at work.

You can also read more about leading 'zoomers' and can purchase additional copies of *Leaderslip* and *ARISE!* at *www.leadzoomers.com.* Join the think-tank around how to lead in a different way in the 21st Century!

BIBLIOGRAPHY

Autry, James A. *Love and Profit: the Art of Caring Leadership.* New York: Morrow, 1991. Print.

Blanchard, Kenneth H., and Spencer Johnson. *The One Minute Manager.* New York: Morrow, 1982. Print.

Buckingham, Marcus and Donald Clifton. *Now Find Your Strengths.* New York, NY: Free Press, 2001. Print.

Collins, James C. *Good to Great: Why Some Companies Make the Leap—and Others Don't.* New York, NY: HarperBusiness, 2001. Print.

Collins, James C. *How the Mighty Fall: and Why Some Companies Never Give in.* New York: Collins Business, 2009. Print.

Covey, Stephen M.R. *The Speed of Trust – The One Thing that Changes Everything.* New York, NY: Free Press, 2006. Print.

Hamel, Gary *The Future of Management.* Gary Hamel, 2007. Print.

Hammer, Michael, and James Champy. *Reengineering the Corporation: a Manifesto for Business Revolution.* New York, NY: HarperBusiness, 1993. Print.

Keirsey, David, *Please Understand Me II – Temperament Character Intelligence.* Matrix Books, 1998. Print.

Peters, Thomas J. *Liberation Management: Necessary Disorganization for the Nanosecond Nineties*. New York: A. A. Knopf, 1992. Print.

Peters, Thomas J. *Thriving on Chaos: Handbook for a Management Revolution*. New York: Knopf, 1987. Print.

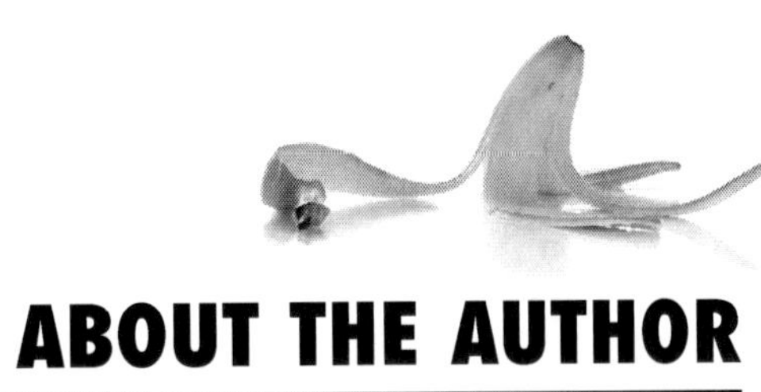

ABOUT THE AUTHOR

Dave Geenens has led numerous business enterprises as President/CEO. Dave's ability to make leaders is the hallmark of his legacy. He is presently investing in future business leaders as the Director of Graduate Business Programs, Director of the Cloud L. Cray Center for Entrepreneurial Services, and is part of the faculty at Benedictine College in Atchison, Kansas.

His first book, *ARISE! Life-changing Truths for the Tormented Leader*, released in 2005, helps enterprise leaders connect the dots between God and work. *Leader*slip is the product of his desire to present fresh, foundational leadership beliefs, paradigms, and practices that leaders can use to transform their enterprises and optimize results.

Dave is founder and CEO of Inhance Leadership, a premier executive consulting and leadership coaching enterprise, focused on making leaders through one-to-one and one-to-few coaching. Dave speaks to enterprise leaders around the country about leadership and its critical role in optimizing results. He and his family currently reside in Overland Park, Kansas.